Message preparation

ANALYSIS AND STRUCTURE

THE BOBBS-MERRILL SERIES IN *Speech Communication*

RUSSEL R. WINDES, *Editor*

Queens College of the City University of New York

GLEN E. MILLS

Northwestern University

Message

preparation

ANALYSIS AND STRUCTURE

The Bobbs-Merrill Company, Inc.

A SUBSIDIARY OF HOWARD W. SAMS & CO., INC.

PUBLISHERS   INDIANAPOLIS   NEW YORK   KANSAS CITY

Editor's foreword

Vital to the preparation of a spoken communication are the processes of analysis and structure. In this volume of the Bobbs-Merrill Speech Communication Series, Professor Mills acquaints the student with both old and new concepts and theories relating to the selecting of subjects for communication, their analysis, their investigation, and their structuring.

Concerning the general considerations involved in selecting subjects, although there is no unique theoretical matter presented, the topical coverage is more thorough than the length of the book may suggest. The selection of subjects in relation to the purposes and types of speeches is extensively treated. Definitions, illustrations, theoretical distinctions, and the findings of relevant research are brought to bear on this topic.

Analysis, which is intellectually the most significant part of speechmaking, is discussed more fully than is customary in textbooks for the first course. The analysis of the kinds of public address is explained theoretically and illustrated. This is an uncommon feature and one that may help to strengthen the academic reputation of the basic course in speech communication.

The chapter on investigating speech subjects is particularly helpful to the beginning student. It is distinguished by the attention given to general or background preparation.

Outlining and the patterns of arrangement are presented in considerable detail. Each principle is demonstrated, and the findings of recent research are cited to modernize traditional theory.

Finally, introductions, conclusions, and transitions are explained and illustrated. This material is a revision of selected chapters from Dr. Mills' **Composing the Speech** (Prentice-Hall, 1952), which is now out of print.

The volume, **Message Preparation,** contains both exercises and bibliography as aids to student use.

Russel R. Windes

Contents

Message preparation

ANALYSIS AND STRUCTURE

Selecting a subject: general considerations

Importance of suitable subject

"What can I talk about?" is a familiar complaint among student speakers. This question is often asked in a way that implies that the rest of the task of speechmaking would be easy if the "right" subject could be found. There is much to be said for this premise. In fact, there are at least four good reasons to account for the importance attached to the suitability of a subject. One is that a subject is the basis of meaningful discourse. Speeches are presumably **about** something, and a worth-while subject distinguishes between a communicator who has something to say and one who merely has to say something. To put it another way, an improper choice of subject often accounts for failure in speech communication. A second reason is that the subject may be a major determinant of audience response. A speaker seeks to affect his listeners in some way, and he hopes his remarks are worth listening to. Interviews and questionnaires have established the fact that listeners consider the choice of subjects to be of essential importance to the effect of a speech. If a speaker nullifies the public expectation, he runs the risk of making himself an object of scorn. A third reason is that a suitable subject stimulates the speaker's desire to communicate and thereby improves his confidence and his delivery in general. It calls forth his best efforts, and it enables him to put more of himself into his speech. He can speak with greater directness and enthusiasm if the subject involves an enthusiasm to be shared or a cause to be championed. Such a subject draws the speaker into the speech and gives it the impress of his own personality. Personal involvement communicates positively, but indifference or detachment communicates negatively. Finally, a good subject motivates more thorough preparation. Intelligence is not enough, and trusting to the inspiration of the occasion is a snare and a delusion. The real effort that competent preparation requires will be less tiresome and more productive if the subject is one that has engaged the speaker's enthusiasm.

Criteria of selection

Here are six guides to the selection of a subject. These are relevant because, as has been stated, a successful speech is purposive in the sense that it is intended to exert some effect upon listeners. Obviously these criteria apply to anyone who selects a speech subject, be he the speaker or someone who assigns subjects. In the latter situation there is less justification for holding the speaker responsible for the outcome. In either situation these priorities obtain.

1. Choose one that interests you and about which you have or can acquire more knowledge than your listeners have. Make your background or general preparation pay dividends. Bring to bear your interests, knowledge, and any other personal resources. In a sense the subject chooses the speaker. It is desirable that a subject be within the speaker's special competence to develop it, but there is no requirement that a student speaker be an "authority" on it.

2. Choose one that the listeners are likely to evaluate as fresh, timely or timeless, and important. Depending upon others for subjects may be less hazardous in relation to this second criterion than it would be in the case of the first, but it is still questionable. It is wise to avoid trite subjects unless you can add a new approach or a new sense of the value of the old. Adaptation to the audience is the key concept here. Remember that interests and values vary among

audiences and even among the same persons from one time to another. Among the significant variables are educational status, social attitudes, interests, ages, vocations, and involvement in the subject under discussion. Even if a certain interest is not active, it may be latent and therefore available for development by a capable speaker. In this connection a beginning speaker is likely to err in jumping to the conclusion that other persons are not interested in hearing his views.

3. Choose a subject that is appropriate to the occasion. In some instances the occasion is a determinant of the choice, but more often the factor of appropriateness or good taste governs. In a speech class appropriateness typically means that the subject fits the assignment. It should also mean that the subject is suitable for a real audience and that a speech class is such an audience. Appropriateness would seem to disqualify Japanese flower arranging as a subject for the main speech at an annual football banquet.

4. Choose one that you can develop in the available time. This means both the time for preparation and the time limit on your speech. Clearly the scope of the subject is involved here. In a five-minute talk, for example, you could not develop adequately an informative discourse on petroleum refining. Difficult, obscure, technical, and complex subjects require more time. It is wise to ask how much time you have, estimate how much you can do in that span, and then stay within that limit. If the intended subject cannot be handled in the available time, narrow the scope, select an alternate, or, unless you are in a speech class, decline the invitation to speak.

5. Choose a single, definite subject. Complex and indefinite subjects are either unmanageable or lead to discursive speech. Speakers are sometimes tempted to branch out into tangential matters unless the subject is sharply limited. An explanation of the latest space vehicle does not require a summary of the history of transportation. It is much better to settle upon one phase and one purpose, especially in a short speech.

6. Choose one that is adaptable to your general purpose. Ordinarily the unlimited subject is selected first, the general purpose second, the limited subject third, and the specific purpose fourth. The choice of materials and their treatment should be in keeping

with the general purpose. Note these steps in the development of the sequence for a longer speech:

Unlimited subject—television cameras for space exploration.

General purpose—to inform.

Limited subject—how an electronics company makes television cameras for space vehicles.

Specific purpose—to explain how R.C.A. made the television cameras for the manned space flights.

Title—How the Man in the Moon Got on T.V.

When we say that a subject should be adaptable to the speaker's general purpose, we mean one of these five general, rhetorical purposes: to inform, to persuade, to inspire, to entertain, and to lead inquiry. These are different from the nonrhetorical or ulterior purposes that motivate some speakers. Suppose a junior executive accepts an assignment to speak to the directors of the company. His general, rhetorical purpose may be to inform his audience concerning the work of his department, but his nonrhetorical purpose, which may actually be the more important to him, is to impress his superiors favorably. Regardless of the importance that ulterior purposes often have, we shall consider only speeches that are intended to achieve one or more of the five general ends or rhetorical purposes. Experience indicates that if a speaker does well with his rhetorical purpose the nonrhetorical purpose will take care of itself.

Thus far in our discussion of rhetorical purposes we have considered only primary ones, but in practice it is possible for a speech to have a secondary purpose as well. The primary, dominant purpose may be to persuade, for example, but there may be a secondary purpose, to inform. Perhaps entertainment is a more familiar situation; it may be the sole purpose, or it may be incidental or secondary, as in a persuasive speech.

In the process of relating his subject to his general purpose, a speaker will do well to consider: (1) the kind of response he wants, either within the listener or outwardly observable; (2) the unit of response, be it individual or group; (3) the duration of the response, whether momentary or sustained; (4) the time of the response, meaning immediate or delayed. The choices should be related to the selection of a specific purpose and to the analysis of subject, audience, and occasion.

Sources of subjects

Your own general preparation, which includes the experiences of your lifetime thus far, is the first source to which you should turn in search of leads to speech subjects. We have seen that together a speaker's knowledge and interests constitute a **criterion** for the choice of subjects. It is equally true that they make up a **source** of subjects. This is obvious in the case of an expert in some field; he is his own best source of material. But what of the so-called typical undergraduate in a speech class? He, too, can draw upon his own knowledge and interests, which have been developed through school, reading, jobs, reflection, and other experiences. Through his choice of subjects for speeches he can share information, insights, experiences, and personal reactions to ideas and events.

The same is true to a considerable degree in the case of a person who has an obviously strong personal identification with his subject: a blind student explaining the training of Seeing-Eye dogs, a former Peace Corpsman urging others to join, a volunteer tutor in a slum discussing poverty, a member of a minority group discussing discrimination, and a homesick student describing his home town or state. There are as many of these strong personal identifications as there are organizations, jobs, beliefs, desires, current events, and the like.

A speaker's own general preparation can serve as a fruitfof source of subjects only if he is alert, curious, interested, and imaginative. Only then can he notice significances, relationships, and applications that he can interpret for others. He should be able, not only to report what he has experienced, but also to analyze what he thinks about it. This requires an alert mind that is interested in ideas, events, people, and things. Traits such as these enable a speaker to select subjects from his own background that will have significance for others as well as for himself.

In addition to his being alert, interested, and communicative, a speaker needs to have a large store of ideas and information gleaned from thinking, observing, reading, studying, conversing, working, playing, and all other facets of general preparation. Worthwhile subjects may be suggested by where a speaker has been, what he has done, what he has seen and heard, what he has thought, and so on. For this reason students are often advised to start their search for speech subjects near at hand: "Cast down your buckets where you are." Everybody has had thoughts and experiences at one time or another. Even if limitations of age and experience may detract somewhat from a speaker's competence, the fact is that no one else can make the best list of subjects for him.

The probable interests of the audience make up another source of subjects in addition to serving as a guide to the choice of a subject. An audience-centered approach requires an objective attitude in a speaker; it involves his asking, "What would the audience in question want to hear discussed?" A speaker who uses this procedure must have enough imagination to project himself into the ideas and moods of others. Common sense should enable a speaker to sense the motives, emotions, attitudes, and expectations of listeners in an after-dinner situation, a between-classes gathering, a protest meeting, or a dedication ceremony. If the audience interest seems to center upon trivia, the speaker should adapt to it with the view toward elevating the goal. Perhaps the listeners can be induced to share some of the speaker's interests. At any rate, many groups will respond favorably to new information, an unusual view of the familiar, or a challenge.

Analysis, adaptation, and projection are fundamental processes. Audience analysis may include taking into account the probable signs of human concerns that can be observed in conversations, speeches, campus publications and meetings, and other local events. Adaptation to these signs and, more importantly, what is behind them is the second step. Finally, there is the projection of the speaker in an empathic sense into an identification with his listeners.

The nature of the occasion is also a source as well as a criterion of speech subjects. Of course there is no element of choice when a subject is either assigned or drawn by lot. But when there is freedom of choice, the nature of the meeting may indicate a subject. Then, too, the speaker's purpose in being present may determine the subject. Meetings occasioned by Red Cross drives, Community Chest campaigns, get-out-the-vote programs, and centennial celebrations, to name a few, clearly indicate certain subjects. Occasions are relevant to practice sessions in speech classes, too. Strictly speaking, the occasion is admittedly just another gathering of familiar faces, but there are other elements such as social events, stories in the campus paper, current rumors, and many other factors. Even so, a scheduled meeting of a class is not as vital as a pep rally, an indignation meeting, or a political campaign. But even if the nature of the occasion fails to suggest a subject, the speaker's choice must be in harmony with the occasion.

Limitation of subjects

The importance of limiting a subject may in some minds be obvious and consequently in no need of elaboration. However, unskilled speakers tend to spread out too far in their subjects, and the results are too sketchy to be effective. They need to say more about less, not less about more. General subjects such as education, mass culture, religion, rebellion, and foreign policy are too broad for short speeches or even single long ones. Limitation can be accomplished by moving from the general to the particular, as in starting with education and limiting the scope to the question of dehumanization in higher education.

Limitations imposed by time are suggested by the preacher's slogan: "No souls are saved after the first twenty minutes." Perhaps an explanation with a wider application would be that many subjects cannot be explained, argued, or otherwise developed in the available speaking time. They must either be narrowed or presented in a series, because each speech should leave a single, clear impression. It is more likely to do so if the specific purpose has been carefully stated and the speech tightly organized. Short speeches are for this reason often said to be harder to compose than long ones.

Limitations imposed by the audience may be so severe as to be prohibitive with reference to specific subjects and individual speakers, but it may be a mistake to conclude that a given subject is inevitably an anathema to a particular audience. The reputation and the personality of the speaker may modify the receptiveness of an audience to a potentially unpleasant subject. For example, a critique of the fraternity system might not be an acceptable subject to an audience of affiliated men if the speaker were a known independent, but it might be tolerated if the speaker were known as a loyal Greek. A second example might be a subject that is supposedly too difficult for the limited background of an audience, because a speaker with unusual skill in informative speaking could conceivably overcome the handicap.

In general, though, we know that the appropriateness of some topics can be seriously affected by such variables as the educational level, intelligence, age, sex, social status, and occupational classification of the listeners. In addition to such variables, the psychology of forgetting needs to be taken into account. A disquieting fact is that only slightly more than one-third of the content of a speech will be remembered after one week. Thus a speaker should select the phases of a subject in which he can reasonably expect to interest a given audience and in relation to which the curve of forgetting will not be ruinous. Audience analysis, at least to the extent of visualizing in advance the persons to be addressed, is obviously important.

Limitations imposed by the occasion are likely to occur to speakers who have at least a normal social sensitivity. Controversial matters are out of place on demonstrative or ceremonial occasions that call for speeches of welcome, tribute, good will, and the like. There are, in fact, many occasions on which some topics within given subjects are inappropriate. Not all are as patently in poor taste as are remarks favorable to atheism in an Easter service. Appropriateness may be a matter of scope, too. There are situations that suggest broad subjects, and there are others that demand narrow ones. Inspirational addresses may at times cover a considerable range, but speeches calling for action must have a specific focus. Listeners should not be left in doubt as to what they have been asked to do.

Limitations imposed by purpose serve to focus the message. If a speaker begins with a general purpose or end in view, he should select a subject and the materials of development in terms of their contribution to that end. If impressiveness is the general end, controversial subjects should be used sparingly if at all. If entertainment is the purpose, subjects that may induce sadness should be avoided. But this does not mean that speech subjects need ever be vague, abstract, or trivial.

Limitations inherent in the speaker himself merit consideration, even though it is difficult to appraise the self accurately. To the extent that it is possible for him to do so, a speaker should select his speech subjects in relation to his interest, knowledge, and general competence. Interest alone is not enough, despite the fact that many speakers bring little more to their subjects, because enthusiasm without content seldom discharges the ethical responsibility of a speaker to his audience.

ASSIGNMENTS

1. List three or four possible subjects for your future speeches. Indicate briefly how well each one meets the criteria of selection, where each one came from, and how you would limit each. The methods of presenting this assignment include oral reports, written reports, and discussions.
2. In a first course in public address, a modified-discussion approach, which is a variation of Assignment 1, may be used to reduce self-consciousness by stressing idea-consciousness. As the students list their subjects in Assignment 1, write them on the chalkboard. Then the class may select three, for example, for further study. After the three subjects have been divided among the class, each student will prepare a three-minute talk on a limited topic under one subject. Thus the subject of superstition could be divided into what it is, the reasons for susceptibility to it, some occupational superstitions, the consequences of the problem, how to cope with it, and so forth. One or two meetings might be used for discussion and speeches on each of the three subjects. One suggestion is to have the instructor and the speakers on one subject seated in a semicircle in front of the rest of the class. For ten or fifteen minutes the leader will stimulate a panel discussion on the general subject. At appropriate points he will call upon individuals to present their three-minute statements. By consulting the outlines in his possession the teacher will know what each student's topic is and where it fits into the general subject.

TWO

Selecting a subject: purposes and types of speeches

For a speech to inform

Nature of informative speaking. Information-giving is probably the most frequent and primary purpose of speechmaking. For this reason the speech to inform is treated here first. It is observable in classrooms, churches, factories, stores, clubs, courts, camps, homes, and on streets, ships, farms, radio, television, and movies. Informative speeches are presented by teachers, lecturers, foremen, leaders, judges, coaches, guides, critics, reporters, preachers, and many others.

Any speech that has as its primary purpose the presentation of a learning experience for listeners is classifiable as informative or instructional. It offers new information, insight, or experience, and its goal is comprehension and probably retention. The learning may be directed toward the correction of ignorance or misinformation, the development of insight, the sharpening of critical faculties, or the acquisition of skill. Speeches of this type are used to define concepts, interpret meanings, analyze and synthesize ideas, classify items, explain relations, review performances, report events, outline procedures, and describe sensory perceptions. Answers ranging from the simplest to the most complex are given to questions such as: How does ACTH act? What is a solid state amplifier? Can a blind person experience beauty? Why do some places have earthquakes? Who may vote in this state?

Subtypes of informative speaking. Four general subtypes can be distinguished, although these categories are not discrete. One is explanatory or instructional. In this group the informative purpose is served by explaining an operation or a process, telling how to do something, or expounding the meaning of a concept. Familiar examples include directions for preparing food, making the factory or the home safe, playing bridge, gardening, and beautifying the female.

A second is called reporting as in treasurers' reports, committee reports, investigators' reports, book reports, news reports, and the like. Reports frequently deal with conditions, events, case studies, financial standing, books, travel, or progress on some project.

Criticizing, evaluating, and appraising constitute the third variety of informative speaking. This sort of oral discourse is typically associated with musical, dramatic, literary, and rhetorical performances. Interpretation and evaluation are undertaken for the purpose of informing audiences.

Lecturing is the fourth subtype, despite the fact that not all lectures are intended to be primarily informative. In the present context, lectures to instruct or inform are included. They are often heard in classes, at conventions, club meetings, and miscellaneous public gatherings. Some lectures are for special-interest audiences, while others are classified as popular lectures.

Although at this point we are interested in instruction as a primary purpose of speaking, we must realize that it is often a secondary purpose of speaking to persuade, to inspire, or to lead inquiry. Thus a legislator explains a bill before he argues about it. There is also the situation in which a speech that purports to be informative is really disguised propaganda. The fact that primary and secondary purposes may become confused, and that a false purpose may disguise the true, places upon both the speaker and his audience the responsibility for keeping the purposes of a speech in their proper relationship, proportion, and focus.

Hints on subjects. In Chapter One, under "Criteria of Selection," six points were made concerning speech subjects in general. Now, with reference to subjects for informative speaking, a few more specific standards will be stated. The first two in terms of importance are listener interest and comprehension. If a subject fills a need, arouses curiosity, or for some other reason appeals to a listener as being worthy of a hearing, it is interesting. Interest, in turn, motivates comprehension, which is the general end of informative speaking. Closely related to these criteria is a third one, which is adaptability to the present knowledge of the audience. The relevant principle of learning is that new information is more readily learned when it is related to prior knowledge by association. Finally, an informative speaker should select subjects that he can treat accurately, comprehensively, and in an orderly way.

For reasons that have been both expressed and implied, it should be obvious that student speakers ought to be given major responsibility for the choice of subjects. Since this is the case, the following list of subjects that college students have used in informative speaking assignments should be considered suggestive rather than prescriptive:

Reading stock quotations	Studying for tests
The Honor Code	Dieting
Programming a computer	How dope addiction develops
Villas and yachts for rent	Door-to-door selling
Detecting counterfeit money	Why humor is funny
Canal dwellers of Thailand	Inflation
Contracts in professional	Using a library
athletics	F.B.I. operations
Development of the income tax	Explanation of modern art
Reviewing a play	Architectural landmarks of
Use of a slide rule	Chicago
Livestock judging	Origins of the liberal arts
Appraising used cars	

For a speech to persuade

Nature of persuasive speaking. Advocatory speaking is the second major type of oral discourse. It encompasses all speechmaking that is intended to influence belief, to evoke action, to modify attitudes or opinions, or to achieve any combination of these effects in relation to controversial subjects. Some theorists distinguish between two ends, conviction and persuasion, saying that the former involves belief while the latter involves action. Conviction is an intellectual response to rigorous argument, according to this view, while persuasion is likely to be a nonrational or an irrational response to emotional appeals and the like.

While it is likely that a thoughtful person can distinguish between the extremes of logical argument and emotional appeal, the fact is that observers in experimental situations have not been able to agree upon the placement of specimen arguments at any points on the continuum of relative rationality. There has been little agreement upon which arguments were "logical" and which were "emotional."[1] One reason is the difference in personal involvement in the subject. Any argument that threatens a person's interests is interpreted emotionally by that person. Moreover, one argument may be both emotional and logical as in the advice that one should not look directly at a solar eclipse lest he suffer retinal damage. For theoretical and practical reasons all advocatory speaking will be classified as persuasive in this book.

Perhaps the nature of persuasive speaking can be explicated further by naming the forms in which it may appear. The types of speeches in which persuasion is most likely to be employed are the deliberative, including legislative and campaign varieties, the forensic, especially the lawyers' pleas, some sermons, and some lectures. Deliberative speakers discuss choices that will affect the future. Their subjects embrace social, political, economic, and philosophical questions relating to the small group, the community, the state, the nation, and the world. When the listeners do something about the proposals, the words are translated into action. Occasions for legislative speaking may range from a local chapter meeting to the General Assembly of the United Nations. Campaign speaking may be either political or nonpolitical, and it may occur as single events or in a series. Forensic speeches are addressed to judges, juries, and commissioners, and they are given under rules or customs of legal procedure. They are basically logical in structure, as are most persuasive speeches intended for critical listeners, but the focus tends to be upon a narrower objective than is the case with either a

---

[1]For a discussion of this problem, see G. L. Cronkhite, "Logic, Emotion, and the Paradigm of Persuasion," **Quarterly Journal of Speech,** L, 1 (February 1964), 12–18.

deliberative or a pulpit speech. Perhaps a revival sermon would be similar to a lawyer's plea in terms of narrowness and immediacy of objective, while the typical sermon has a longer-range goal. Finally, those lectures that are intended to influence behavior toward controversial conclusions are classified as persuasive. In all of these applications of persuasive speaking, the subjects are called **propositions.**

Nature and kinds of propositions. Persuasive speeches are given to influence choices, and this implies rivalry between or among the possible choices. Rivalry in this form is known as **controversy,** the basis of which is best expressed in a proposition. In political speaking a proposition might be a declarative sentence such as "John Doe should be elected Mayor" or "Vote 'yes' on the school bond issue." In forensic speaking the basis of the controversy is stated in the prosecutor's charge or the plaintiff's complaint. A lecturer or a preacher might address himself to an ethical proposition—in this instance stated as a question, "Is the Good Samaritan out of date?" Propositions in legislative meetings are expressed in the form of motions, resolutions, bills, and ordinances.

There is not only variety in the forms in which propositions are stated; there is also variety in the kinds or classes of such statements. The reason for classifying propositions is that each type has distinctive proof requirements and must therefore be analyzed differently. For the moment, however, we are concerned only with the selection of subjects for persuasive speeches. In this connection six kinds of propositions will be identified and illustrated:

Proposition of legal fact—X slandered Y.

Proposition of past fact—Slavery was not a direct cause of the Civil War.

Proposition of present fact—The party in power is to blame for the crime rate.

Proposition of prediction—Curtailment of foreign travel will strengthen the dollar.

Proposition of value—American foreign aid is wrong in principle.

Proposition of policy—Professional boxing should be outlawed.

Sources and wording of propositions. Under what circumstances might a person or a group become identified with a proposition? One is a situation in which a problem gives rise to one or more proposed solutions in a meeting. In this setting a proposed solution is a motion or a proposition. Another source could be a person's reaction to some disturbance, as in the case of a citizen's advocating an ordinance to prohibit jet flights in certain localities. A third source could be the circumstances of one's job or of his involvement in some activity. Thus when legislation to control firearms was introduced, thousands of spokesmen for rifle clubs rushed to the defense of their hobby.

Whenever a spokesman has his choice of a proposition to attack or to defend, he should observe four criteria. One is significance, which means that the subject is worthy of discussion. Another is that the problem be suited to the persuader's interest, knowledge, and belief. Third, the proposition should be potentially interesting to the expected audience. Finally, the subject matter should be appropriate to the occasion.

Even though a persuasive speaker may not elect to divulge his proposition in so many words, he needs a carefully worded proposition for his own guidance. This is a technical matter in the study of argumentation, but here it will be simplified for nonspecialists. If a speaker intends to oppose a specific proposal, his declaration should say so in a clear and simple declarative sentence. Next, a proposition should express the view of a dissatisfied party, thereby placing the burden of proof upon the side that affirms the proposition. If the speaker in question desires to oppose the proposition as worded, he is obviously on the negative side. Third, a proposition should contain one idea only. A student speaker might advocate the honor system for his college (if it did not have such), but he would be in error if he urged at the same time the adoption of an honor system **and** a four-quarter calendar.

Problems of analysis and proof. At this time we shall not deal with the complexities of analysis and proof. Instead, we shall concern ourselves only with the importance of isolating and classifying propositions. A would-be persuader cannot determine what he must prove if he does not know what his proposition is. If his subject is only a catch phrase instead of a complete idea, he cannot define terms, find issues, determine his responsibilities for proof, or choose his supporting materials intelligently. As we shall see in Chapter Three, each kind of proposition has its distinctive proof requirements. Proving that X slandered Y is vastly different from proving that fraternities should be abolished.

Some propositions for persuasive speeches.
Legal-fact propositions include changes such as these: (1) Z
Company conspired to restrain trade. (2) Mr. Sparrow killed Mr.
Robin. (3) Miss X is guilty of arson. (4) Mrs. Y ignored the
traffic signal at ––– on –––.

Past-fact propositions include assertations of this sort: (1) In
World War II the Allies were not in complete accord on the
objective of unconditional surrender. (2) Tobacco chewing was
once a popular habit. (3) Greed was the undoing of the Roman
Empire. (4) A newspaper campaign set off the Spanish-American
War.

Present-fact propositions include claims like these: (1) The
cost-of-living index is at an all-time high. (2) There are no atomic
secrets. (3) Most British physicians oppose the national health
service. (4) The Ku Klux Klan does not exist in Alabama.

Predictive propositions include these and similar controversial
forecasts: (1) Federal grants will distort the development of education. (2) This course will make you a better speaker. (3) Our
recognition of East Germany would drive West Germany out of
NATO. (4) Unrestrained consumer credit will increase the cost of
living.

Value propositions include evaluative judgments such as these:
(1) Television is a vast wasteland. (2) Divorce laws are anti-
quated. (3) Uncle Sam is a poor businessman. (4) Betting is
morally wrong.

Policy propositions include urgings of this sort: (1) The U. S.
should get out of the U.N. (2) Relief rolls should be publicized.
(3) Attend the Mock Political Convention. (4) Quit smoking today.

For a speech to inspire

Nature of inspirational speaking. A speaker's purpose is to inspire or to impress, or his general end is inspiration or impressiveness, when he tries to make his audience feel either a favorable or
an unfavorable attitude more intensely. Sometimes this sort of public address, as in some sermons and lectures, is called "stimulating." The purpose is to make the listeners feel deeply the value of
certain virtues, principles, institutions, persons, or ideas. As we

shall note in more detail later, this purpose is observable in eulogies, keynote addresses, and in inspirational speeches for sales meetings, banquets, campaign rallies, commencements, Memorial Day, and kindred occasions. These demonstrative speeches are traditionally divided into the courtesy and the commemorative varieties. Courtesy speeches include introduction, farewell, welcome, presentation, commencement, dedication, response, and acceptance. Doubtless the most familiar commemorative speeches are the anniversary, the eulogy, the tribute, the dedication, and the inaugural.

Themes for inspirational speeches include, for example, pride in the past, optimism for the future, praise or blame, and the virtues of loyalty, sacrifice, unity and confidence. In order to select the most suitable theme for inspiration, a speaker must achieve a closer identification with his audience than the so-called typical speaker ever does. He needs to know what they have certain feelings toward, and he needs to know the nature of those feelings. Thus if the speaker is not a member of the group, his audience analysis will have to be considerable.

Relation to other purposes and types. Inspirational speaking is in some respects the most difficult to understand. It is related to persuasion in that it may be preparatory to action, or it may be generalized, deferred action. A speech advocating a specific act of courage would be persuasive, but a talk on the courage of Joan of Arc would be inspirational or impressive. Another way to express this difference is to point out that, although an inspiring address is persuasive in that it modifies attitudes, it only reinforces them; there is no disagreement to reduce. In other words, the speaker adapts to existing attitudes and heightens them. For a similar reason it is said that entertaining speaking and inspirational speaking are related; both are intended for emotional impact, albeit of different sorts.

Three cautions stem from the discussion of the relationships between inspirational speaking on the one hand and persuasive and entertaining speaking on the other. Inspirational speaking is more difficult to do in the sense of avoiding sentimentality, colloquially known as "corny" material. However, the tradition calls for more polished style and delivery, especially on ceremonial occasions. Finally, the audience often comes closer to determining the content of this type of speech, because there must be no disagreement in point of view or general tone.

Specimen subjects. Commemorative speeches, sermons, and lectures have been given on these and similar inspirational themes: Easter, Christian martyrs, ideals of Thoreau, fighters for freedom, Mother's Day, the founding fathers, school spirit, moral courage of Senator Norris, Brotherhood Week, and Fourth of July. Specific farewell addresses that come readily to mind include those of President Washington, King Edward VIII, and Abraham Lincoln at Springfield. Daniel Webster at Bunker Hill and Lincoln at Gettysburg gave distinguished dedicatory addresses. Ingersoll's "At His Brother's Grave" is a eulogy that has been widely printed and recited. Inaugural addresses by presidents and governors are, of course, familiar to most of us. Finally, the category of inspirational lecturing can be represented by Wendell Phillips' "The Lost Arts" and Russell Conwell's "Acres of Diamonds."

For a speech to entertain

Nature of entertaining speech. Although this is usually treated as one of the minor types or kinds of public address, it is not inconsequential or easy. To entertain means more than merely to arouse interest, for all speeches are expected to do that. It is the more difficult task of showing an audience a good time throughout the speech. At least this is the situation when the primary purpose of a speech is entertainment. We say that some entertainment is useful in most speeches for the reason that attention can be attracted or renewed by wit, humor, suspense, and the like, even when entertainment is only a secondary or an incidental purpose.

Entertaining speakers help listeners to pass the time pleasantly, to relax, and to get their minds off their cares. Their remarks may or may not be funny, or they may be diverting because they offer vicarious thrills of adventure or absorbing accounts of human interest. Either a covert response like quiet attention or an overt one such as a smile or a laugh may be the desired response. Both responses are immediate and fleeting; there is no obligation upon the listeners to continue their responses after the speech. If the chosen medium is humor and the audience is sophisticated, a light touch is preferred to the broad, slapstick variety; heavy, forced, or abusive humor is more likely to antagonize. But whatever kind of material the entertaining speaker uses, the pleasure experienced by the listeners takes precedence over the logical rigor of the discourse. The speech may even be nonsense, but it is more likely, as in the case of an after-dinner speech, to have a unifying theme that makes sense.

Problem of finding a subject. You might infer from what has been said above that finding a subject for an entertaining speech is difficult, and so it is for many students. One reason is the misconception that entertainment requires humor. Another is that few subjects are inherently amusing; it is the manner of treatment that makes the difference between a serious talk and an amusing one. One characteristic of this manner of treatment is the adaptation to the background and understanding of the audience in order to insure quick comprehension. If the selected manner of treatment is humorous, the techniques of incongruity, irreverence, and satire become likely choices. If it is mostly nonhumorous, then travel, adventure, and human-interest materials are appropriate. In both cases the skills of narration and description are of crucial importance.

Specimen subjects. Anthologies of speeches contain a few specimens of this genre: Mark Twain's "Settling the Corset Problem," Harvey T. Harrison's "Whither Midst Falling Due," Chauncey Depew's "Pilgrims in Holland," George Ade's "Toast to Sir Thomas Lipton," and Robert Benchley's "The Treasurer's Report," for example. These are titles some of which reveal their subjects. In the following list, however, there are some students' subjects without titles:

Training a puppy	Parachute jumping
The kitten that chose me	Interesting cultural differences
Potato-peeling technique as a personality index	Door-to-door selling
	Unusual occupations
Excuses traffic cops hear	To Europe on a shoestring
Why horses don't bet on people	Outmoded laws
Mistaken identity	Living with parents
Life in a small town	Unforgettable characters
Types of dates	National parks
Art of bluffing	Frustrations of childhood
Folk tales of a region	Spring-vacation migration of students
Deep-sea fishing	
Mountain climbing	Solving a mystery

For a speech to lead inquiry

Nature of inquiry. In its broad sense, inquiry can mean analysis and investigation by an individual or a group. Within the context of oral communication, inquiry can be conducted in a group discussion, or it can be led or initiated by a single speech. Because of its comparative rarity, the single speech of inquiry may fairly be said to be a minor type. Inquiry through group discussion, though, is much more widely practiced. In either format, inquiry proceeds from questions toward answers that are not predetermined. Any speaker who leads or induces inquiry has something in common with informative and persuasive speakers; he prepares and motivates his audience to seek answers to his questions. He also serves as a sort of one-man discussion group in that he brings up essentially the same topics, stages, or questions that a problem-solving group deals with in its process of reflective thinking.

Subjects for inquiry. Unless some matters are proscribed as being unfit for discussion, we may say that any problem or question is suitable for inquiry if the audience can at least make progress toward answering it in the available time, if the problem is of interest, and if options are available. Subjects for inquiry can be classified in the same way as propositions for persuasion. The major difference is that inquiry starts with a question while persuasion starts with an answer. This can be demonstrated by recasting one of the six specimen propositions into a question: "American foreign aid is wrong in principle" becomes "Is American foreign aid wrong in principle?" Immediate dichotomization into "yes" and "no" camps is the obvious weakness of this procedure. Inquiry would be better served by phrasing the question this way: "How should we evaluate our foreign aid program?"

Other questions of fact, of value, and of policy may come to mind as one reacts to current affairs. This is a question of fact: "What is the truth about smoking in relation to health?" This is one of value: "How good is our school system?" This is one of policy: "What should be done about classroom cheating?"

ASSIGNMENTS

1. Each student will come prepared to suggest one speech subject for each of the five rhetorical purposes. Greater variety will be achieved if

the subjects are chosen from various categories, such as international, national, local, and personal. International and national subjects need not be political; they may be ethical, philosophical, cultural, or social. Personal subjects should be more significant than petty grievances. They may deal with a woman's goal in a profession dominated by men, the question of postponing marriage for education and employment, or personal reactions to customs, social values, or taboos.

2. Prepare and deliver an extemporaneous, informative speech on a subject of practical or of mainly intellectual value. The emphasis may be upon "how to do it," "what to do in case of . . . ," or "what it means." Submit an outline before you speak. (See the form that follows.) An open forum after each speech can be used to judge comprehension, attitudes, and so forth. The critique form, which also follows, may be used if desired.

3. Adapt Assignment 2 to a speech to persuade. Shift-of-opinion ballots may be used with this exercise.

4. Speeches to inspire, to entertain, or to inquire may be assigned if desired.

PRELIMINARY SPEECH OUTLINE

*Name*_____*Section*_____*Date*_____

*Subject*_____

*General Purpose*_____

*Specific Purpose*_____

*How Subject Was Limited*_____

*Why Subject Was Chosen*_____

Opening Statement

Main Topics

Closing Statement

CRITIQUE FORM

Listener's Name _____

Section _____ *Date* _____

Speaker's Name _____

Subject of Speech _____

_____

General Purpose _____

Specific Purpose _____

_____

Six Criteria of Subject Selection:

    1. *Which one was met best?*

_____

    2. *Which one, if any, was not well met?*

_____

Apparent Source of Subject _____

_____

How Well Was Subject Limited? _____

_____

Evaluate the Suitability of This Subject to the Purpose and Type of Speech (Informative, Persuasive, etc.)

_____

_____

_____

Was Specific Purpose Achieved? Explain Decision.

_____

THREE

Analyzing a subject

Nature of analysis

When a speaker analyzes a subject, he takes it apart, in an intellectual sense, in order to probe its meaning or to discover what topics are involved. He seeks not only to discover topics or "talking points" but also to trace their relations to the subject and to each other. He performs this operation chiefly by raising questions that will reveal the significant aspects of the subject. This process is preliminary to outlining in that it leads to the discovery of the specific purpose, the main points, the subpoints, and their interrelation.

After a speaker has settled upon the general purpose of his speech (to inform, to persuade, to inspire, to entertain, or to lead inquiry), his next step is the statement of his specific purpose. Suppose the general purpose were to inform and the subject were how to read stock quotations. The specific purpose might be stated thus: "To teach my classmates how to read the New York Stock Exchange quotations in the metropolitan dailies." Or suppose the purpose were to persuade and the subject (proposition) urged the curtailment of foreign travel for the purpose of strengthening the dollar. The specific purpose of an affirmative advocate would be something like this: "To persuade my audience that we should try to curtail foreign travel in order to strengthen our dollar in international exchange." A negative advocate would very likely try to show the folly of the proposal.

After a speaker determines his specific purpose, his next step is to select the main ideas or principal divisions of the subject which, once they are developed, will suffice to achieve that purpose. In the instance of each of the five types of speeches there are characteristic topics or questions, as will be illustrated below. They may be chosen in terms of either objective or psychological considerations, although these bases are not mutually exclusive. Objective considerations are subject-centered, while psychological considerations are audience-centered.

Importance of analysis

People who regard speechmaking as a significant intellectual activity, rather than the practice of sophistry, rank analysis at or near the top in priority. Only through analysis can a speaker determine which ideas are relevant and important to his subject and his purpose. In fact, superficial and rambling remarks are likely to occur when a speaker, even if he has a purpose, proceeds without having thought out a procedure for achieving it. Herein lies the greatest risk of impromptu speaking.

There are even more specific reasons for attaching so much importance to the analytical process: it enables a speaker to investigate his subject with discrimination and judgment; it helps him to limit his scope; it is a prerequisite to outlining. Discerning analysis improves the investigation of a subject because it guides the selection of materials that will serve the purpose of the speech. Knowing which points or topics are vital to his subject and his purpose, a speaker can seek materials that will support those points. He will know what he needs and will be able to recognize appropriate material when he sees it. Perhaps even before he seeks material he will be well advised to limit his subject, and he can do this through a preliminary analysis. Take the case of a general subject on arbitration of labor-management disputes, the preliminary analysis of which reveals economic, legal, political, social, and moral topics. If it seems unwise to discuss all five topics, the speaker must choose fewer and limit his talk accordingly. Thereafter he can better organize his speech, because analysis is a prerequisite to outlining. Analysis precedes synthesis, which in this context means that a person preparing a speech takes his subject apart before he puts his speech together.

General procedures

Beginners sometimes ask which should be done first—analysis or investigation. Generally speaking, the best answer is that preliminary analysis should precede and consequently help to guide the reading which, in turn, may provide leads for deeper analysis. Take the instance of the general subject, arbitration of labor-management disputes, stated above. Having found economic, legal, political, social, and moral topics by means of preliminary analysis, the next step is to investigate through reading or some other means the available material on each topic. Aided by new information or fresh insight, the preparing speaker could then select the most promising of the five topics and analyze each one more thoroughly to get at the suitable subtopics which, in turn, would be investigated by means of reading, observing, interviewing, or other appropriate procedures.

Three stages of general procedure have much favorable experience to recommend them. First, while taking a mental inventory of what you know and think about the subject, or during your observing, reading, or conversing, start a random list of points that come to mind. Second, select a basis of grouping the listed items: space, time, simple-to-complex, problem-solution, comparison-contrast, cause-effect, or correlation, for example. Finally, group the related topics under these broader headings in preparation for outlining the speech. Suppose the subject for an informative speech were interesting places to visit in Chicago. A random list of points might look like this: (1) Adler Planetarium, (2) Art Institute, (3) Board of Trade, (4) Natural History Museum, (5) City Hall, (6) Marina City, (7) Lincoln Park, (8) Museum of Science and Industry, (9) McCormick Place, and (10) Newberry Library. One basis of grouping these miscellaneous items might be kinds of interests: scientific, artistic, financial, political, architectural, and so forth. Another scheme might be regional: North Side, South Side, West Side, Lakefront, Loop, and so forth. In either case the ten particulars would be grouped under appropriate headings. Instructions on how to adapt these procedures to each of five kinds of speeches will now be explained and illustrated.

For speeches to inform

Theory. According to the traditional theories of topical analysis, there are some stock questions with which a speaker may begin his mental inventory: Who? Which? What? When? Where? How? and possibly Why? If the purpose is to explain **how** or **when,** the next likely step is to ask yourself whether a time sequence, as in the consecutive steps in a process, or a series of topics of degree will serve. In case **where** is the central question, a spatial or geographical order becomes a likely choice. Questions of **who, which,** and **what** often call for the definition and the clarification of existential details plus the determination of criteria for judging those details. Topics concerning the existence, substance, or form of persons or things also have potential relevance. But the clearest way to explain some schemes of topical analysis for informative speeches is to cite illustrations from practice.

Practice. Speaking on "The History of the Concept of Freedom," Ralph H. Lutz used these six topics in a time sequence:

1. Why is individual freedom a vital subject today?
2. Where or with whom did the idea of freedom originate?
3. How did the idea develop abroad?
4. What happened to the idea in early America?
5. How has the American example influenced the world?
6. What are the threats to freedom today?

In his speech, "The Historian's Job," Gilbert Highet explained three types of history: memories, reconstructions, and imaginative descriptions.

Speaking to the Bond Club on how the American Telephone and Telegraph Company serves the public, Walter S. Gifford used three topics: (1) It performs a nationwide service. (2) It maintains high standards of quality control. (3) It is an extensive business enterprise.

It is not surprising that Nicholas M. Butler saw fit to use these five topics of information in his lecture, "Five Evidences of an Education":

1. Correctness and precision in the use of English.
2. Refined and gentle manners.
3. Power and habit of reflection.
4. Power of growth.
5. Efficiency, or the power to do.

John Ruskin's lecture on "work" was developed from four topics based upon distinctions among industrious persons:

1. Between the workers and the players.
2. Between the producers and the consumers of the means of life.
3. Between those who work with their heads and those who work with their hands.
4. Between those who work wisely and those who don't.

For speeches to persuade

General theory. Audience analysis, which is obviously important in preparation for persuasive speaking, is treated in another volume in this series. Suffice it to state here that one should analyze his audience at least enough to determine whether it is generally apathetic, opposed, or neutral, because each attitude requires different adaptations. The obvious reason is that some of the potential points will be more effective than others in arousing interest, reducing opposition, or encouraging commitment.

Substantive analysis, as distinguished from the analysis of audience or occasion, is the intellectual process of determining what a speech subject means and what controversial questions must be answered if the treatment is to be logically adequate. In persuasive speaking, subjects are technically known as propositions, and the controversial questions are called issues. The answers that an advocate elects to make to these issues are his points-in-partition or "talking points." Finally, when a speaker has arrayed his points and has amply supported them with evidence, reasoning, motive appeals, and possibly other forms of support, then he has "made his case."

Each kind of proposition poses its own problems in analysis; but before these specifics are taken up, the analysis of one general proposition will be demonstrated. Suppose a speaker planned to advocate the withdrawal of American forces from Viet Nam. His analysis of the proposition might induce him to set out all or some of these points, depending upon available time, available material, audience interest, and possibly other relevant considerations: (1) The situation is a civil war in which we have no right to interfere. (2) The people don't care whether or not they live under communism if they can live in peace. (3) We can't fight for democracy by backing somewhat undemocratic regimes there. (4) The leader of North Viet Nam may become an Asian Tito. (5) Escalation of the war pushes Russia and China closer together. (6) Asia is not of vital interest to us.

A discerning analysis need not yield several points as in the preceding case. Consider, for example, how a pacifist might advocate the same proposition, namely, that the United States should withdraw from Viet Nam. He might argue only two points: (1) Our involvement is war. (2) War is the worst crime against humanity. These two advocates of the same proposition would start from different premises in the form of assumed values or criteria. One function of analysis is the determination of such basic premises.

Specific theory and practice. One who would analyze a controversial subject (proposition) concerning an alleged past fact, present fact, or future fact (prediction) needs to ask at least two exploratory questions: (1) What is the nature of the fact, or what are its necessary elements? (2) Were these elements present, or are they present, or will they be present? Let us see how these analytical questions might be applied to the propositions listed in Chapter Two. Take the allegation that slavery was not a direct cause of the Civil War. Incidentally, the "negative" wording is justified if the advocate is opposing the prevailing view. In this situation the advocate might raise these preliminary questions: (1) Under what circumstances would slavery be disqualified as a cause of the war? (2) Were these circumstances in effect at the time? Or he might ask more specific questions: (1) Would a direct cause have been discussed as such by the opposing leaders? (2) Did they fail to discuss slavery in that context?

Next, take the allegation that the party in power at City Hall is to blame for the crime rate. Three preliminary questions that could lead to further analysis are: (1) Has the crime rate grown worse under the present administration? (2) Has the administration failed to take remedial action? (3) Are crime rates a reflection of the effectiveness of local government?

Moving to an allegation of future fact, otherwise known as a controversial prediction, consider the proposition that the curtailment of foreign travel will strengthen the dollar. Do expenditures by Americans abroad weaken the dollar significantly? Would travel restrictions halt this trend? Can we be sure that no side effects of a travel ban would upset our calculations? These are likely questions when one begins to analyze a controversial prediction of this sort. Obviously an affirmative advocate answers "yes" to all crucial questions such as these, while a negative must answer "no" to one or more of them.

In the instances of propositions of value the analytical questions relate to criteria and their application. Anyone who intends to charge that American foreign aid is wrong in principle will be well advised to ask what errors of principle might relate to programs of foreign aid and whether our program is affected by such errors. Such general queries might lead to these more specific questions or issues: Is an aid program wrong in principle if it fails to insist upon honest administration? Does our aid program fail to require this? Is an aid program wrong in principle if it fails to require ideological agreement with us? Does our aid program fail to require this? Is an aid program wrong in principle if it does not insist upon economic reforms? Does our program fail to do this? These are some of the actual issues in contemporary public discussions of foreign aid.

Another proposition of value can be seen in the primary campaign plea that John Doe would be a well-qualified candidate for mayor. After having raised the analytical questions on criteria and their application, an affirmative spokesman might adopt these points or topics: (1) John has leadership ability. (2) He is experienced in local government. (3) He enjoys a good reputation. (4) He knows how to interest people in their local government. If the proposition were one of policy, that is, to nominate John Doe, one would probably add a fifth point: He can win.

Propositions of policy are characterized by calls for action or by the urging of solutions to problems. An opponent of a proposition is said to be on the negative side. He would add "not" to the affirmative statement of the proposition. The operation of this principle can be seen in a dispute over the fraternity system. Since the system exists, any advocate who would abolish it must express his proposition affirmatively, that is, in language calling for abolition: "College fraternities should be abolished." The negative would think in terms of this proposition with "not" added between "should" and "be."

Preliminary analysis might begin with these exploratory questions: (1) What does the proposition mean? (2) How did the problem develop? (3) What criteria should any solution meet? (4) How does the present situation measure up to those criteria? (5) What are the possible solutions? (6) Which solution will most adequately meet the criteria?

In case an advocate has the problem and his favorite solution clearly formulated, he may dispense with the preliminary, exploratory questions and move directly to the potential issues. These are vital questions on which the controversy should turn. Some version of these two questions constitutes the minimum responsibility of an affirmative side: (1) Are there serious and inherent faults in the present situation? (2) Is the affirmative's proposal the best solution? The foregoing questions are called stock issues because they are abstractly worded so as to fit all manner of policy propositions. In actual practice an advocate would be well advised to express these issues in terms of his proposal. If it were the abolition of fraternities, for instance, the two broad stock issues might be worded as follows: (1) Do fraternities interfere with the intellectual involvement of students? (2) Would the benefits of abolition outweigh the possible disadvantages of such action?

Advocates who are inexperienced in analyzing propositions of policy or action may profitably begin with four narrower questions instead of the two broad ones. Potentially important considerations are less likely to be missed if this is done. Stock questions such as these can be revised to fit a specific proposition of policy: (1) Does a problem of some consequence exist? (2) Does it stem from remediable causes? (3) Does the proposal offer a remedy? (4) Will this remedy be desirable in terms of cost, freedom from harmful side effects, and superiority to other remedies? If the proposal called for a change from a quarterly calendar to a semester plan, the four stock questions might be adapted as follows: (1) Is the quarterly calendar hard to live with? (2) Are these irritations directly attributable to the length of a quarter? (3) Would a semester division alleviate these irritations? (4) Would it be worth the inconvenience of changing? and perhaps (5) Would this be better than a trimester plan?

For speeches to inspire

General theory. Proceeding from the analysis of the major types of speeches, the informative and the persuasive, to that of the comparatively minor forms, we shall begin with the analysis of speeches to inspire, impress, or stimulate. Communications of this sort may appear as sermons, popular lectures, commemorative and dedicatory addresses, eulogies, remarks of welcome and farewell, inaugural addresses, and other so-called occasional speeches. It is appropriate to move from the analysis of persuasive subjects to that of inspirational subjects because these two types have some elements of persuasion in common.

Inspirational speaking is somewhat persuasive in that it reinforces existing attitudes, feelings, and values, but the strategy is more amplificatory than probative. Consequently, audience analysis becomes more vital than substantive analysis, and most certainly the "stock" approaches that apply to advocatory messages are inappropriate here. It is better to select topics or points the listeners know and then to apply the values or criteria they will accept. Thus we may conclude that there is less inventional latitude in the analysis of inspirational subjects because of the ritualistic context and the consequent expectations of those present. There is some challenge, though, and it comes in finding fresh or original ways to amplify the familiar topics.

Specimens of analysis. Lincoln's Gettysburg Address epitomizes a temporal analysis. It begins with the past ("Fourscore and seven years ago. . ."), shifts to what was then the present ("We are met on a great battlefield. . ."), and closes with a reference to the future (". . . that this nation, under God, shall have a new birth of freedom. . .").

President Charles W. Eliot of Harvard, speaking to the alumni on Commencement Day, 1898, followed an introducer who spoke of the financial cost of the Spanish-American War as being large enough to support 365 Harvards. Eliot's central idea was that then, as ever before, Harvard was discharging her duty. His lesser topics were three: (1) Educated youths who love their country do not consider in what precise cause their country has gone to war. (2) They go to war for a variety of simple reasons. (3) Universities must go on through peace and war. If you question this analysis, try to judge it in terms of the climate of opinion of 1898. Even then you may wonder how the speaker knew his first and second lesser points were factually sound.

Henry W. Grady's inspirational speech "The New South" used a comparison-and-contrast scheme of analysis. After contrasting the South of slavery and secession with that of union and freedom, he compared North and South on the basis of things in common.

In his speech accepting the Nobel Award, William Faulkner developed two main themes: that man is immortal and that the writer's duty is to help man endure by reminding him of his past glories that have made life meaningful. In the process of reaching these themes, he touched upon three lesser topics: (1) I use this moment of acclaim to catch the attention of young writers. (2) Young writers have forgotten the problems of the human heart in conflict with itself. (3) They must write of love, honor, pity, pride, compassion, and sacrifice.

The Reverend Dr. Ernest F. Tittle's commencement address at the School of Speech, Northwestern University, in 1924 was titled "Learning To Speak." Apparently the speaker had asked two analytical questions: Why is speech important? What do I mean by "learning to speak"? He gave three answers to his first question: (1) Speaking helps one to clarify his own thinking. (2) Good speaking is a pleasure to hear. (3) Speeches by the famous and also by the ordinary have made history. His reply to his second question constituted the major portion of the address, and it was actually a lecture on rhetoric.

Finally, Raymond B. Fosdick's inspirational speech at the dedication of the Mount Palomar telescope used a dilemma-resolution analysis of the title, "The Challenge of Knowledge." Four main topics were used. (1) Knowledge and destructiveness have joined in a kind of Grand Alliance. (2) One cannot predict the uses knowledge will serve. (3) We must seek ways to deal with our modern dilemma. (4) Our sick world needs an astronomer's perspective.

For speeches to entertain

General theory. After deciding upon entertainment as the purpose and choosing a suitable subject, the problem is how to treat the material entertainingly. This is because pleasure, not substantive merit, is the usual test of this kind of speaking. Particularly in after-dinner and other humorous speeches, manner counts for more than matter. Thus it follows that a would-be postprandial speaker needs to analyze not only the audience and the occasion but his own talents most of all. If he doesn't have the gift of wit, he had better leave the after-dinner speaking to others.

In case he decides to try his hand at this sort of speaking, there are several schemes of analysis and organization from which to choose. He might take a single, simple idea or theme and elaborate upon it with illustrations and stories. Or he might give the same idea a full treatment with irony or mock seriousness. Still another possibility is the master illustration that may require several minutes to make the intended point. In any case the after-dinner speech should be brief, vivid, fast-moving, and witty without being embarrassing. Numbered among the familiar devices of support are burlesque, exaggeration, understatement, satire, and the unexpected "twist."

Not all entertaining speeches are humorous, however. Many travelogues are sold as entertainment, but humor is typically a minor ingredient. They are more informative than funny; yet they are accepted as entertainment. This fact suggests that the speaker might quite properly analyze his travel subject as if it were for a speech to inform, except that he would consider how to make his material entertaining. Persons who give travelogues for a living cannot afford to ignore this principle the way many amateurs do.

Specimens of analysis. When Congressman John Allen of Mississippi spoke humorously in the House of Representatives on "Appropriation for a Fish Hatchery," he invented three topics which, by themselves, give no hint of his cleverness. He touched upon the importance of tupelo in American history, its importance to both North and South in the Civil War, and its importance in terms of economics. It is in the cleverness of his exaggeration rather than in the nature of his topical analysis that the explanation of his success is to be found.

Mark Twain's response to the toast, "To the Babies . . .", given at a banquet sponsored by the Army of the Tennessee for General Grant in 1879, used one central idea: "It is a shame that for a thousand years the world's banquets have utterly ignored the baby, as if he didn't amount to anything." He selected two points with which to develop his theme: (1) a description and narration of a baby's taking over a household, and (2) the possible futures of some of the present babies.

Speaking at a banquet of the Indiana Society of Chicago in 1908, Booth Tarkington addressed himself to the title, "Where We Come From." He used four related topics in good-naturedly developing the common bond: (1) He made fun of his own public-speaking experiences. (2) Nobody ever really quits being from Indiana. (3) Kentuckians exaggerate their state's virtues, but Hoosiers don't need to. (4) We're proud to be called Hoosiers.

Chauncey M. Depew, who was probably the most widely known after-dinner speaker in his day, spoke on "The Pilgrims in Holland" to the New England Society of Brooklyn. He, too, used four topics: (1) The pleasures of attending dinners given by various nationality groups. (2) The special pleasures of a New England dinner. (3) Peculiar traits of the Puritans. (4) Yankees who learned some things while in Holland made the United States the great nation that it is.

"Whither Midst Falling Due?" was the title of Harvey T. Harrison's address to the Mortgage Bankers Association of America in 1936. This speech combined entertainment with a conservative attack upon the New Deal, taxes, federal power, and the like. Its first three topics were a jocular reference to the introducer, a comment upon the etymology of "Mortgage," and a humorous exaggeration of the speaker's adventures with a mortgage. Next came the serious themes: (1) Since the coming of the New Deal, how unfashionable it is to pay your debts, (2) What the onset of the Great Depression was like, (3) The lamentable taxation we suffer, (4) The problem of retarding the erosion of local government by growing federal power.

These illustrations show the absence of any standard patterns of analysis that are applicable to subjects for entertaining speeches. There is, for instance, nothing remotely resembling the stock issues that are available for use in analyzing propositions of policy for advocatory speaking. Lacking such preliminary guides, a speaker who hopes to entertain an audience must rely mainly upon his sense of humor.

For speeches to lead inquiry

When several speakers engage in a problem-solving discussion using what has come to be known as **reflective thinking,** they are likely to use some adaptation of John Dewey's pattern of inquiry: (1) location and definition of problem, (2) description and limitation of problem, (3) suggestion of possible solutions as hypotheses, (4) testing and evaluation of proposals, and (5) selection and implementation of a solution. This pattern of analysis for use by discussion groups was popularized by the McBurney-Hance **Principles and Methods of Discussion**[1] in 1939, and it has influenced much of the literature since that time.

Quite recently a few theorists[2] have posited the idea that an individual speaker may have occasion to address an audience on some problem without presuming to advocate one solution. For instance, a city manager might start a council discussion of what to do about downtown traffic congestion by giving a speech based upon the first three of Dewey's five steps. In a sense this would not be a completed speech; it could be described as a speech in process. Its objective would be to prepare and motivate the audience to finish the deliberative process.

Speaking to foment and lead inquiry resembles informative speaking in some respects and persuasive speaking in others. It is informative in that it provides the data with which to begin, and it would be indirectly or implicatively persuasive if the single speaker proceeded through to one recommended solution. Any so-called inquiry speech that does not give the audience some options at the end is nothing but disguised persuasion.

If **one** speaker were to present the variety of views on movies and

[1] J. H. McBurney and K. G. Hance, **The Principles and Methods of Discussion** (New York: Harper, 1939).
[2] James H. McBurney and Ernest J. Wrage, **The Art of Good Speech** (Englewood Cliffs: Prentice-Hall, 1953), chap. 13; John F. Wilson and Carroll C. Arnold, **Public Speaking as a Liberal Art** (Boston: Allyn and Bacon, 1964), chap. 7.

censorship that four participants actually expressed in a "Small World" telecast moderated by Edward R. Murrow,[3] we should say that, if the speaker concluded by inviting the audience to choose among those views, he would have given an inquiry speech.

If the speaker were in a problem-solution situation in which a policy or an overt action were at stake, he might analyze his subject with these questions: (1) What is the problem? (2) What causes have produced the problem? (3) What criteria or values are applicable to any proposed solution? (4) What solutions are possible? (5) What may my audience decide when solutions are evaluated, combining steps three and four?

ASSIGNMENTS

1. One general subject such as movie censorship could be used by the class for this exercise. Individuals or groups might be assigned so that one works on a speech to inform, one to persuade, one to lead inquiry, and possibly one to entertain. Each person or group would analyze the subject in relation to his assigned purpose and would invent the essential topics or "talking points." Comparisons of the several analyses should be instructive.

2. Each student should prepare a speech on a subject of his own choice. The preparatory notes, which could be called in for inspection prior to the delivery of the speech, should explain the method of analysis and list the points to be discussed.

3. Descriptive, critical analyses of speeches that have been read or heard will be given for the purpose of reporting the apparent analysis (list the points made) and evaluating its adequacy.

[3]Carroll Arnold, Douglas Ehninger, and John Gerber, **The Speaker's Resource Book** (Chicago: Scott, Foresman, 1961), p. 121.

FOUR

Investigating a subject

Investigation defined

Sometimes acquiring information about a speech subject amounts to nothing more than skimming a magazine article or asking someone a few questions, but it can mean a diligent inquiry that deserves to be called research. Thinking, observing, listening, conversing, reading, corresponding, and taking notes are the familiar activities that fall within the category known as investigation.

Investigation is related to analysis, which was discussed in Chapter Three, in that both are facets of specific preparation. Although the processes are related, analysis means the discovery of the topics or "talking points" within a subject, while investigation is the process of finding the materials with which to develop those topics.

Speakers conduct investigations or research their subjects for the purposes of accumulating a background of information, refining their analysis, finding evidence and illustrations, uncovering principles, locating the bases of comparisons, learning relevant events, and in other ways discovering and evaluating the materials that can be used in developing their points. Without doing this, most speakers should not expect to be worth hearing.

Primacy of general preparation

Most of us think of investigation in relation to the preparation of a specific speech, the subject of which has been chosen. There is, however, an important sense in which preparation is general, which is to say that it is a lifetime process of making oneself worth listening to, and it is not pointed toward any specific speech. The primacy of general preparation means that a speaker's background or general competence belongs in first place, both in time and in order of importance.

"My whole life is a general preparation," said Henry Ward Beecher, an eminent preacher and lecturer. Another famous American speaker, Daniel Webster, expressed a similar view while commenting upon his celebrated "Reply to Hayne": "I felt as if everything I had ever seen or read or heard was floating before me in one grand panorama, and I had little else to do than to reach up and cull a thunderbolt and hurl it at him."

"But I'm no Beecher or Webster," a student may protest. True, a novice speaker must usually begin with little general preparation, but he can strive to remedy his immaturity. The excuse of youth wears thin in time. Creativity and the integration of ideas take time; they cannot be achieved through the reading of a few popular magazine articles. Accomplished, mature speakers do not do all of their speech preparation after they have decided to speak on a particular occasion. They realize, as beginners must, that audiences are more likely to respond to speakers who are thoroughly qualified. There is no easy short cut; the road to rhetorical excellence is arduous.

Broad, general education, whether formal or informal, is one dimension of general preparation. It implies learning how to think, cultivating discriminating tastes, and exposing oneself to experiences that contribute to growth. In the ancient days of Isocrates and Cicero, the ideal speaker was thought to be one who knew something about almost everything, and everything about the subject of his speech. Nowadays we cannot reasonably demand so much, but we do expect more than a veneer of sophistication. For the college student this implies that he should get the most out of his academic opportunities.

Observation is a second constituent of general preparation. Creative speakers, composers, and writers have eyes that see and ears that hear—just as other people do— but theirs seems to work more efficiently. Such persons are sensitive to their environment, and they show perspicacity in their discernment of relationships and implications. Through observation, a speaker finds leads to subjects, topics, and illustrations. In fact, a speaker's discourse reveals what he has experienced and what those experiences have suggested to him. This is how the power of imagination comes into play. Abraham Lincoln and many other speakers with little formal education had to depend heavily upon this power.

Closely akin to schooling and observation is the habit of discriminate reading. This helps a person to understand persons and events by opening for him the thoughts and actions of individuals and societies of all ages. As Bacon said, "Reading maketh the full man." Numerous biographies and dissertations document the claim that reading has contributed much to the speeches of eminent persons from Edmund Burke to Winston Churchill, to name but two.

Even if a person reads much, he cannot expect with certainty to recall at some future date every appropriate item he may wish to use. Lacking the memory of a Webster, he must adopt some system of note-taking and filing. Students are, therefore, often required to keep scrapbooks, card files, loose-leaf notebooks, or other repositories of information. Before James Madison ever spoke on the Constitution, he prepared from his long study a comprehensive set of notes, written on small, folded papers, which formed a compact booklet he could carry in his pocket.

These primarily intellectual attainments are important but insufficient resources. The most competent speakers have often been emotionally responsive as well as intelligent. They have wide sympathies and keen sensibilities, which are popularly known as "personal magnetism." Knowledge of and feeling for one's fellow men broadens the sympathies, supplements the academic attainments, and enables a speaker to adapt his remarks to his listeners. In this connection the careers of Henry Clay, Harry Emerson Fosdick, and Clarence Darrow come to mind.

Certainly vocabulary and general command of the language should be included among the desirable attributes of a speaker. A speaker needs a copious vocabulary in order to achieve clearness, interestingness, and accuracy of statement, but he should not use his vocabulary for purposes of display. These techniques have been found helpful: trying to cultivate an interest in language development, forming the habit of noticing new words or effective combinations of words in the writings and speeches of others, using new locutions until they become familiar, habituating the use of a dictionary, and studying languages. Woodrow Wilson told how his father insisted upon a careful choice of words. It is also a matter of record that Lincoln, Webster, and others consciously worked to improve their English usage.

Practice in speechmaking was a part of the general preparation of major figures in the history of public address. John Calhoun practiced intensively while in law school, Wendell Phillips at Harvard, Beecher at Amherst, Henry Grady at the University of Georgia, and many others, including Albert Beveridge, in intercollegiate oratory. Many who attended preparatory schools and colleges in the nineteenth century studied the rhetoric of oratory in credit-bearing courses. Leaders in British public life for generations have been veterans of university union (intramural) debating. The role of practice can be summed up in Winston Churchill's testimony: "The truth is that I am not a good speaker and I only learned to speak, somehow or other, with exceptional difficulty and enormous practice."

Despite the apparent decline in writing as a mode of preparation, it must be reported that the diligent practice of writing stimulates thought and improves the orderliness, accuracy, finish, and power of expression. Cicero's advice on writing as the best teacher of oratory can still be read with profit by the enthusiasts for the **ad lib**: "No orator will ever attain the highest success without long and continued practice in writing, however resolutely he may exercise himself in extemporary speeches."

Next among the many varieties of general preparation are two seemingly incompatible items, solitude and travel. Leading speakers have mingled with people the better to know them, but they have also at times enjoyed "creative solitude." It was Webster who wrote, "And when **thinking** is to be done, one must of course be alone. No man knows **himself** who does not thus, sometimes, keep his own company." He and others have also testified that visits to new places can supplement reading as a source of new ideas.

Finally, the development and the disciplining of a creative imagination deserves mention as an aspect of a speaker's general preparation. This is basic to creative endeavor in the practical arts as well as the fine arts. Imagination in the practical art of public speaking is important because it accounts for the development of impelling images in discourse. By this device a speaker makes his audience "see" things beyond their own experiences. He can project himself into the life experiences of others, and this enables him to put ideas into images that others can see or feel. Whenever a speaker's performance shows evidence of skillful analysis, apt illustration, impelling motivation, or language facility, imagination has been at work.

Specific preparation: general hints

Once a person knows he has a speech to make, he must shift from general to specific preparation. Perhaps his first question is **when** to conduct his investigation. It makes a difference whether the subject is assigned by someone, drawn by chance, or selected by the speaker. Contestants in extemporaneous speaking do not phrase their subjects, and their time for specific preparation is limited to an hour or less. Consequently they perform a quick analysis, take a mental inventory of their ideas and information, and peruse whatever notes or printed materials the rules allow. All other kinds of specific preparation are simply out of the question. If, on the other hand, a speaker has a free choice of subject, he may select a general subject and a general purpose, make a preliminary analysis to guide his further study, undertake some of the investigative procedures explained below, phrase a specific subject and a specific purpose, refine his analysis in the light of his findings, and continue his investigation in terms of the final subject, purpose, and topics or points. In short, he uses analysis and investigation alternately.

The importance of investigation should be obvious to all but the stupid, the lazy, or the incredibly conceited. A person who is already expert in a subject understands the importance of investigation even though he does not need to do more of it in preparation for a specific speech. Back of this conclusion are the premises that listeners with good sense expect a speaker to know what he is talking about, and that ethical speakers do not face audiences unprepared.

In this connection it may be useful to distinguish between original and unoriginal investigation. The former is first-hand inquiry as in interviewing, conducting experiments, sending out questionnaires, or making observations on a field trip. Unoriginal investigation is more often done by student speakers. They typically locate and cite reports made by other persons who conducted the original investigation. Students are usually advised to concentrate upon unoriginal investigation except in the instances of purely personal or local subjects.

If a speaker aspires to excellence, though, he should work for originality and thoroughness. Those speakers who have ample self-discipline investigate competently, give credit to their sources, and add their **own** reactions or interpretations to the materials. Teachers have this in mind when they advise students to "put more of **themselves**" into their speeches.

Miscellaneous procedures

As mentioned earlier, a speaker's background is often his greatest potential resource when he begins to investigate a specific subject. Thinking about that background is, therefore, a likely first step, and it may occur in the form of taking a sort of mental inventory of what one knows and thinks about the subject. Speakers who take time to survey their own thoughts before they turn to other sources are more likely to excel in originality. Reading is important, but it is not a good substitute for thinking.

When previous personal experiences do not suffice, it is possible to turn to original or first-hand inquiry in the form of questionnaires, correspondence, personal observations, or surveys. Data from these sources lend freshness and credibility to illustrations and evidence. But only when other sources are inadequate is it advisable to impose upon other persons with letters or questionnaires. Visits to observe what one plans to talk about, such as slum housing, can be illuminating and accomplished without inconveniencing other people.

A third category of miscellaneous investigative procedures includes conversations, interviews, discussions, speeches by others, movies, and broadcasts. Preparing speakers use conversations and interviews to learn what others know or think about their subjects or to try out their ideas on a few listeners first. The best way to learn what views some professors hold toward fraternities is to ask them. Sometimes the best way to explore a complex subject that can be divided among a few students is to have a round-table discussion on it. In all of these procedures efficient listening is essential.

Keeping up with current affairs is either general or specific preparation, depending upon the purpose. The **New York Times,** the **Christian Science Monitor,** the **Wall Street Journal,** and a few other major dailies will serve most general purposes. The **National Observer** and perhaps some weekly news magazines serve to provide more perspective than the dailies. Finally, there are monthly and quarterly journals intended for a considerable variety of general and specialized interests. These are a few that will serve to illustrate: **Harper's, Fortune, Monthly Labor Review, Foreign Affairs,** and **Annals of the American Academy of Political and Social Science.**

Using libraries

Reference works are of many kinds, ranging from the extremely general to the most highly specialized. General guides such as Winchell's **Guide to Reference Books** lead to the more specific references. They serve to answer a specific question such as, "Where can I find material on 'right-to-work' laws?" Guides to newspapers and periodicals, **British Union—Catalogue of Periodicals,** for instance, serve an obvious purpose. Probably the most familiar general periodical index is the **Readers' Guide to Periodical Literature.** It is used to locate magazine articles on a wide variety of subjects. Among the specialized periodical indexes are **Art Index, Biography Index, Book Review Digest, Education Index,** and **Publishers' Weekly.** Newspaper accounts of events can be traced by subject or name of writer in a newspaper index, notably that of the **New York Times.**

Bibliographies, biographical references, encyclopedias, yearbooks, dictionaries, government documents, pamphlets, and dissertations also belong in the reference category. Bibliographies are lists of materials on specific subjects. Occasionally they are annotated, meaning that the nature of the contents is briefly noted after each item. There are even bibliographies of bibliography—Besterman's **World Bibliography of Bibliographies,** for example.

Biographical references include **Who's Who in America, Contemporary Authors,** and **Directory of American Scholars.** For general background information turn to an encyclopedia such as the **Britannica,** but for specialized interests consult encyclopedias in social science, government, education, or other fields. Yearbooks that contain accounts of events in specific years include **World Almanac, Statistical Abstract of the United States,** and **Information Please Almanac.** In addition to the general dictionaries, there are specialized ones, such as those which cater to the interests of lawyers, physicians, and other specialists. There are so many government documents besides the **Congressional Record** that several guides are published. In the field of pamphlets and leaflets there are in excess of forty thousand items, many of which can be located through the **Vertical File Index** and **Public Affairs Pamphlets.** In case an undergraduate wishes to consult a dissertation on the subject of his speech, he can trace it through **Dissertation Abstracts,** a monthly listing. If an item seems to be promising, it can usually be obtained in microfilm.

   Card catalogues in libraries of any significant size are divided into general and serial sections, and the entry cards are filed alphabetically in the long sliding trays.

   In the **General** catalogue books are listed by the author's name or, if no author is named, by the title of the work. Authors can be persons, institutions, or branches of government. Interfiled among the author cards are entries for titles, subjects, and secondary authors. Subject headings appear at the top of a card, either in red or in black with red underlining. Cross references, of which there are many, are filed at the end of a subject. A list of these may be found in the Library of Congress, Subject Cataloging Division, **Subject Headings.**

   Serial catalogues hold cards for bound periodicals, such as **Harper's,** and society publications in a numbered series, such as **Quarterly Journal of Speech.** In the latter case a journal is more likely to be found under the name of the society. Each card shows which volumes and numbers of a given serial are in the library's holdings. The recent issues, however, are probably shelved in a periodical room, while the bound volumes are stored in the stacks.

   In the context of speech preparation, **how to read** is not a matter of elementary literacy. It is a matter of planning, progression, and attitude. Suppose your intended speech subject concerns state "right-to-work" laws. Prior to limiting this subject for a single-speech purpose, read on the general subject of labor legislation—its recent history, its political connections, its economic and moral implications, and so forth. This suggests the use of a plan of reading based upon the questions raised in the preliminary analysis of the subject (Chapter Three). The most general references such as an encyclopedia might be consulted first, followed by textbooks in economics, specialized books in labor legislation, and finally the professional journals, the **Congressional Record,** and similar sources. The point of this progression is that the investigator proceeds from the general, secondary sources to the specific, primary sources of information. It is better to cite an opinion of the Supreme Court than to quote a columnist's interpretation of it. Likewise, the best source of Senator X's remarks on a bill before the Senate is the **Congressional Record,** not a publication of an interested organization.

Speed, discrimination, and assimilation are characteristic of efficient reading for information. Material that is less than vital in terms of its relevance to the topics or points discovered through the analysis of the subject can be skimmed, while the most useful material will be carefully studied with the view to taking notes. But it is not enough merely to gather interpretations, facts, and illustrations. These are but raw materials that need to be evaluated, related to other data, and interpreted in terms of the speaker's purpose. Reading is thus an active process; it involves noticing not only **what** was said but also **why.** Moreover, it is best done with an alert, open, and inquiring mind.

Finally, there is the matter of taking notes. Extensive notes and an elaborate filing system are necessary in preparing for extemporaneous speaking contests, a season of school debates, or even a series of speeches on a general subject. In the situation of most classroom speakers, however, the notes tend to be so few and for such immediate use that a file-card system is seldom required unless it is an extension of the general-preparation procedure. Four common-sense hints have been found widely useful: put only one item on a card or a sheet, write a headline-type caption at the top to identify the topic, document the source, quote accurately.

ASSIGNMENTS

1. Continue the first or second assignment at the end of Chapter Three. Add investigation notes that may be used in developing the points found by analysis. Label each note to indicate which subtype of general or specific preparation it represents.
2. Continue the third assignment at the end of Chapter Three. Evaluate the information and identify the subtypes as in the first assignment above.
3. Prepare a short, annotated bibliography and one note card of information from each entry. These will presumably be used in a future speech.

FIVE

Outlining and patterns of arrangement

Theory of outlining

There are two main purposes in outlining speeches: to aid the speakers and to aid the auditors. From the speaker's viewpoint, outlining is an aid to preparation as well as to presentation. In fact, some speakers habitually make two outlines for a speech, a detailed one for preparation and an abridged version for presentation.

A preparation outline is particularly useful in that it arranges the materials in an orderly fashion. It is an organized storehouse of ideas. When it is correctly done, it helps the speaker to observe in perspective the main lines of thought, the relationships among the several parts, the adequacy of the forms of support, and the unity, coherence, and emphasis of the speech as a whole. This procedure can sharply reduce the incidence of omissions, digressions, inconsistencies, unsupported assertions, and misplaced emphasis.

A presentation outline can help a speaker to recall materials, to keep them in the intended order, to apportion his time efficiently, and to adapt to audience attitudes. These benefits accrue only when the presentation notes are brief, clear, and structured so as to capitalize upon association of ideas. Probably only the fourth benefit requires explication—how careful planning enables a speaker to adapt the unfolding of his ideas to the audience attitudes that he has found through his analysis of the situation. This can be illustrated with reference to the first two sections of Webster's celebrated speech "The Constitution and the Union." Perhaps at no other time in his forty years of speechmaking did Webster exert so much effort to adapt in this way. Since the Northern and the Southern Senators were contending bitterly over the Fugitive Slave Law, Webster faced two nearly irreconcilable attitudes. Realizing this, he opened his speech with a short introduction consisting mostly of ethical appeal, or remarks to bolster his credibility. Following this, he gave a long narrative sketch of the history of the problem and prepared the way for his appeal to compromise.

While it is significant that a presentation outline can help speakers, it is probably more important to know that it helps listeners. Support for this conclusion could be drawn from rhetorical theory and from experimental research, but only the latter will be cited here. Smith's study of the effects of speech organization upon attitudes[1] showed that, when at least two main parts of a speech were transposed, the difference in persuasiveness was significant. Over-all organization seemed to be an important factor in persuasion when the influence of organization upon comprehension was investigated. However, it is worth noting that disorganization was achieved for the compared group by moving paragraphs about. An earlier experiment found that organization showed no marked superiority to disorganization when measured by comprehension of the message.[2] In a later experiment the same investigator[3] found a slightly more favorable effect of organization upon comprehension. He had asked, "Do audiences that hear disorganized materials make their own organization and consequently remember the material better?" The finding was negative, because the organized speech more often resulted in better comprehension. However, organization showed no statistically dependable superiority over the disorganized. In rela-

[1]Raymond G. Smith, "An Experimental Study of the Effects of Speech Organization upon Attitudes of College Students," **Speech Monographs**, XVIII (November 1951), 292–301.
[2]K. C. Beighley, "An Experimental Study of the Effect of Four Speech Variables on Listener Comprehension," **Speech Monographs**, XIX (November 1952), 249–258.
[3]K. C. Beighly, "An Experimental Study of the Effect of Three Speech Variables on Listener Comprehension," **Speech Monographs**, XXI (November 1954), 248–253.

tion to the retention of information, though, the superiority of the organized speech was shown.[4] Organizational structure made a difference in immediate retention scores. The level of ability to organize possessed by listeners also affected retention. An experiment that involved reading rather than listening indicates that disorder reduces clarity.[5] This study of sentence order and comprehension shows that the shifting of sentences out of their logical order in a fifteen-item outline affects comprehension adversely and that the amount of loss increases with the degree of disorganization. Finally, the research on informative speaking has been scanty, but several studies indicate a general superiority of organized learning over the poorly organized. It must be conceded, however, that the role of structure is inconclusive, both in informative and in persuasive speaking.[6]

What has been said of the purposes of outlining applies to informal remarks as well as to prepared speeches. Many persons mistakenly think that speeches for which there has been little specific preparation do not need any organization. Informal remarks, in this view, are supposed to be offhand ramblings. The fact is that there is often a low level of efficiency in disorganized speech. Some students have become more effective in short-notice, informal remarks by learning and using a few simple patterns of arrangement: problem-solution, time order, simple-to-complex, and others in this chapter.

The kinds of outlining are typically described in the literature of public address, the logical and the topical. In a logical outline there is one essential relationship among the ideas: each subpoint must contribute toward **proving** the point to which it is immediately subordinated. The following sequence of ideas from a speech by Carl Schurz on civil-service reform illustrates this necessary relationship:

    I. There is need for civil service reform, because
        A. abuses exist in the present method of appointments to office, and
        B. the spoils system has an adverse effect upon the individual and the body-politic.

[4]E. C. Thompson, "An Experimental Investigation of the Relative Effectiveness of Organizational Structure in Oral Communication," abstract of dissertation in **Speech Monographs**, XXVII (June 1960), 94–95.
[5]D. K. Darnell, "The Relation Between Sentence Order and Comprehension," **Speech Monographs**, XXX (June 1963), 97–100.
[6]C. R. Petrie, Jr., "Informative Speaking: A Summary and Bibliography of Related Research," **Speech Monographs**, XXX (June 1963), 79–91.

This relationship that obtains in argumentative outlines should be indicated, as in the specimen above, by the word **for** or **because.** The word **and** connects coordinate points, meaning those of comparable rank. To test the logical adequacy of this kind of outline read it from top to bottom, stressing the connectives, and then from bottom to top, substituting **therefore** for **because.** If both readings make sense, the outline is probably sound. Moreover, this kind of outlining may be used for both refutory and constructive arguments.

Topical outlining is distinguished from the logical in that the subpoints **explain** or **illustrate** the points to which they are immediately subordinated. In many cases the relation between a topic and its subtopics is that of the whole to its parts. Because of its non-argumentative thought relationships, topical outlining is well adapted to exposition, narration, and description.

There are also compositional differences between logical and topical outlining. Complete sentences are not required in topical outlining; words and phrases will usually suffice. Furthermore, the connectives, which are optional in this situation, differ from those of logical outlining. Instead of using **because,** it is possible to use **namely, as follows, in that, for example,** and the like. The following specimen of topical outlining was used for an expository talk on "What Goes into a Speech":

I. Personal experiences
   A. To lend authority
   B. To improve directness
II. Examples or illustrations
   A. One every few minutes
   B. Make us see a point
III. Comparisons
   A. Lend interest
   B. Clarify ideas

IV. Visual aids
   A. Kinds
   B. Values
   C. Limitations
V. Light touch
   A. Kinds
   B. Values
   C. Risks
   D. Hints on use

Types of outlines, of which there are four in this discussion, are distinguished mainly by the comparative length and complexity of their points and subpoints. The first and simplest is the list of words. It is too sketchy to serve as a preparation outline unless the speaker is experienced and the subject is familiar. If the lack of supporting details in a word outline does not prove to be a handicap, a speaker may use it as a presentation outline after he has made a preparation outline. This is a list-of-words outline:

Leading Features of Our College
1. Faculty
2. Admission policies
3. Financial resources
4. Physical plant
5. Academic offerings
6. Activities programs

Next is the **phrase** outline that consists of a series of topics and subtopics expressed in key phrases or short statements that are less complete than sentences. Each phrase, in theory at least, contains essential, easily remembered expressions that suggest ideas, moods, and a vivid impression of reality. The specimen topical outline of "What Goes into a Speech" is also a phrase outline.

This type of outline is well suited to exposition, description, and narration. In fact, many experienced advocates have used it in the narrative, descriptive, and expository subpoints of their argumentative speeches. Beginners are cautioned against the possible overlooking of logical relationships in the hybrid type of outline. Then too, a phrase outline requires more skill in thinking on your feet, because the phrases must be expanded into sentences and perhaps paragraphs during the act of speaking.

Sentence outlines are the most complex of those that emphasize structure. Less experienced speakers, in particular, are advised to make sentence outlines, although they should learn to deliver their speeches from briefer notes or without any notes. This kind of outline is so named because each topic and subtopic is written as a complete sentence. All six general principles of outlining must, of course, be observed.

Sentence outlines require careful preparation, which may be the reason why teachers often require this type. Such an outline, when learned, most effectively reduces the danger of forgetting the ideas. For the reasons explained in relation to logical outlining, a sentence outline is almost a necessity in argumentative speaking. The specimen of logical outlining from the Carl Schurz speech is also an example of a sentence outline. It exemplifies the strict, logical relationships that proof demands, but sentence outlines that are not designed to prove may have a looser relationship among their points.

Structure-substance outlines are used for descriptive and critical analysis of speeches. They are more often used in the process of analyzing other persons' speeches for the purpose of identifying the speech materials that were used in the composition. Students are sometimes required to make preparation outlines of this type so that they can indicate where and how they have utilized the assigned varieties of speech materials. The left side of the page contains the structural outline of the speech, while the right side is used for substantive identifications. Space limitations dictate a limited scope for any one outline. The following specimen is based upon the introduction and the first main point of "Against the Compromise of 1850" by Jefferson Davis:

Introduction

I. It must be the cause, and not the advocate, which has filled the floor and the galleries of the Senate today.

Plea for attention: reference to urgency of problem.

II. I am grievously disappointed in the conduct of the Senator (Clay) from Kentucky.

Effort to achieve ethical persuasion: attacked Clay's motives and integrity.

A. He has sided with the strong against the weak.

B. He has denied to slavery that protection guaranteed by the Constitution.

Metaphorical statement of purpose: "I now come to lift the glove he then threw down."

Discussion

I. The attack upon the South must be arrested.

No partition or transition. States the problem.

A. The attack endangers the Union by its threat to the domestic peace and social relations of the South.

Aims at Southern alarm.

B. The attack is being furthered by unconstitutional means.

Aims at Northern sympathy.

1. It encourages the federal government to assume powers not granted.

Not strong in evidence and reasoning thus far.

2. It threatens to destroy the necessary balance of power between the sections.

General principles of outlining apply to all of the kinds and types discussed above.

Simplicity. Six fundamental principles must be observed in either logical or topical outlining. The first of these is simplicity, which means that each unit in the outline should contain only one idea or statement. Observe the difference between the "right" and "wrong" specimens in this respect.

(*Wrong*)	(*Right*)

I. Married women should not be allowed to work for pay because their husbands support them and many of them have inheritances; besides, unemployed men and unmarried women need these jobs, and married women let their outside work interfere with their duties at home.	*I. Married women should not be allowed to work for pay, for*
	  A. They do not need to earn money, for
	    1. Their husbands support them, and
	    2. Many of them have inheritances.
	  B. Their jobs are needed by others, for
	    1. Some men are unemployed, and
	    2. Many unmarried women have to support themselves.
	  C. Outside work interferes with their home duties.

Coordination. This principle means that a series of topics must have a generic relationship. In other words, the points must have one or more important elements in common. The placing of a foreign or an unrelated idea in an otherwise homogeneous list constitutes a violation of this principle.

(*Wrong*)	(*Right*)

I. Protestant churches in our town
  A. Methodist
  B. Presbyterian
  C. Catholic
  D. Baptist
	I. Protestant churches in our town
	  A. Methodist
	  B. Presbyterian
	  C. Baptist
	II. Catholic churches in our town
	  A. St. Athanasius'
	  B. St. Mary's

Subordination. Most college students know that outlines have main points and subpoints. The "right" example immediately above involves the subordination of the A-B-C points. Supporting points that bear some common relationship are subordinated to a superior point. Degrees of subordination are indicated by symbols and amounts of indentation.

<table>
<tr><td>(Wrong)</td><td>(Right)</td></tr>
<tr><td>I. Uses of a lawn mower</td><td>I. Uses of a lawn mower</td></tr>
<tr><td> A. Cuts grass</td><td> A. Cuts grass</td></tr>
<tr><td> B. Provides exercise</td><td> B. Provides exercise</td></tr>
<tr><td> C. Problems of maintenance</td><td>II. Problems of maintenance</td></tr>
<tr><td>   1. Adjustments</td><td> A. Adjustments</td></tr>
<tr><td>   2. Sharpening</td><td> B. Sharpening</td></tr>
<tr><td>   3. Lubrication</td><td> C. Lubrication</td></tr>
<tr><td>   4. Proper storage</td><td> D. Proper storage</td></tr>
</table>

Discreteness. Each topic or point in an outline should be a separate and distinct idea. It is a mistake to allow any points to overlap, merge, or otherwise become indistinct or confused. In the next example note that D overlaps other points in the "wrong" specimen.

<table>
<tr><td>(Wrong)</td><td>(Right)</td></tr>
<tr><td>I. How to seed a lawn</td><td>I. How to seed a lawn</td></tr>
<tr><td> A. Rake the ground</td><td> A. Rake the ground</td></tr>
<tr><td> B. Sow the seed</td><td> B. Sow the seed</td></tr>
<tr><td> C. Apply fertilizer</td><td> C. Apply fertilizer</td></tr>
<tr><td> D. Prepare the soil</td><td> D. Roll the surface</td></tr>
<tr><td></td><td> E. Water regularly</td></tr>
</table>

Sequence. Ordinarily it is wise to arrange the coordinate points in some sort of significant order or progression, as suggested in the section on "Patterns of Arrangement." Some of the more common sequences are those of time, space, problem-solution, simple-to-complex, and so on. When one pattern is decided upon, there should be no deviation that would impair its effectiveness.

<table>
<tr><td>(Wrong)</td><td>(Right)</td></tr>
<tr><td>I. Evolution of group life</td><td>I. Evolution of group life</td></tr>
<tr><td> A. Family</td><td> A. Family</td></tr>
<tr><td> B. Clan</td><td> B. Clan</td></tr>
<tr><td> C. Town</td><td> C. Town</td></tr>
<tr><td> D. State</td><td> D. State</td></tr>
<tr><td> E. Nation</td><td> E. Nation</td></tr>
<tr><td> F. United Nations</td><td> F. League of Nations</td></tr>
<tr><td> G. League of Nations</td><td> G. United Nations</td></tr>
</table>

Symbolization. Each point in an outline should be marked by a number or a letter symbol that indicates the relative rank of that item in terms of coordination and subordination. Points having similar symbols are expected to be of comparable importance in the hierarchy of speech materials. It is well to adopt one set of symbols for use in all outlining. The most common practice is to use Roman numerals for main points, capital letters for the first series of sub-points, Arabic numerals for third-level points, lower case letters for the fourth, and so on. Only one symbol per point is permitted. Furthermore, if the statement of any point requires more than one line, all lines after the first should have the same indentation as the first line. Both errors appear in the "wrong" specimen.

<table>
<tr><td align="center">(Wrong)</td><td align="center">(Right)</td></tr>
<tr><td>I. A world government would solve the international peace problem, for</td><td>I. A world government would solve the international peace problem, for</td></tr>
<tr><td>I.A. It could succeed even if one country opposed it, for</td><td>A. It could succeed even if one country opposed it, for</td></tr>
<tr><td>A.1. The process of proposing it and the likely adoption of it would show up any recalcitrant as a potential aggressor.</td><td>1. The process of proposing it and the likely adoption of it would show up any recalcitrant as a potential aggressor.</td></tr>
</table>

Patterns of arrangement

The importance of a pattern is sometimes underestimated. Let us assume that a speaker has chosen his subject, analyzed it, investigated it, and determined its purpose. He then needs to partition and organize the materials of the speech. Accomplished speakers have found that this task is made easier by dividing the materials according to a consistent method or principle. This involves viewing the speech materials from one point of view, such as time, space, and so on.

While outlining a speech consider carefully the problem of proportion, or the amount of time which each part of the speech will be allowed. Failing to do this, a speaker may find that his allotted time has elapsed before he has treated some essential point. Even if a badly proportioned speech is finished on time, it may leave a mistaken impression concerning the relative importance that the listeners are supposed to attach to certain points.

Arrangement, in a broad sense, means the major, over-all division of speech materials into introduction, body, and conclusion. But since the special problems of introductions and conclusions will be discussed in the next chapter, the present concern is with the techniques of arrangement that apply more especially to the body or discussion part of a speech. These techniques are comprehended by the patterns of arrangement that apply to the disposition or ordering of the materials in the body. The number and the diversity of these patterns suggest that there is no all-purpose scheme that will serve all occasions.[7]

Some kind of pattern is a practical necessity for three reasons: it is a normal outcome of discerning analysis; it is a prerequisite to clear outlining; it makes for a consistent point of view. Suppose that a person were preparing a speech on the summer recreational facilities in the Chicago area. His analysis might lead him to ask, "What are they, and where are they?" Either the "where" or the "what" would become the basis of an arrangement. In case the former were selected, the pattern would be the space order; in case the latter were used, the pattern would be topical classification. In one case the main points would deal with places and the minor points with activities, while in the other case the order would be reversed. This hypothetical situation illustrates the emergence of a pattern as a result of analysis, the usefulness of a pattern in the process of disposition or arrangement, and the consistency in point of view that a pattern provides.

Time order obviously refers to an arrangement of topics according to a forward or a backward progression in time. It is not limited to the old stand-by, past-present-future. Narrative materials such as historical and biographical sketches, personal experiences, and the like lend themselves to a temporal sequence. But the time order alone is likely to result in a mere string of incidents unless the patterning of subtopics follows a more penetrating scheme such as causation or some other. Five possible points for a speech on the history of flight are arranged here in a time order:

[7]Paul E. Reid, "A Spectrum of Persuasive Design," **Speech Teacher**, XIII (March 1964), 87–95.

I. Balloon ascensions
II. Propeller-driven planes
III. Jet aircraft
IV. Unmanned spacecraft
V. Manned spacecraft

Space order, or the spatial pattern of arrangement, is based upon places, geographical divisions, or parts of an object. It is used most often with descriptive matter, but it is useful whenever a subject or some part of it deals with material that has spatial relationships. The most orderly method is to select a suitable point of departure or a vantage point, such as east, left, top, end, and so forth, and to proceed with the places, parts, or objects in the order of their positions in space.

Such a spatial progression makes for clearness through visualization, but it should not be used mechanically or uncritically. It may be that the spatially related items have other and more vital associations such as relative importance, association of ideas, or increasing complexity. Mood-creating description, for instance, is more effective when arranged according to suggestive details instead of a strictly spatial order. In the next specimen outline the points are spatially ordered under the title, "What the World Thinks of Our Foreign Policy."

I. Western Hemisphere
II. Non-Communist Europe
III. Africa
IV. Non-Communist Asia

Implicative order is the name given to that pattern of arrangement which presents all but the speaker's conclusion to a controversial problem. Listeners are left to draw the conclusion that the speaker has implied. In theory, a questionable or a seemingly unacceptable conclusion has a better chance of acceptance if the listeners are led through a series of related points the acceptance of which will imply the truth or the wisdom of the implied conclusion. In other words, a broad context is treated as a thought-whole consisting of a series of topics so related by implication that the acceptability of one is implied by the credibility of the preceding ones. The implicative order may be called a "chase" technique, because the speaker leads the audience in pursuit of one solution after another until the final one is reached by a process of elimination, otherwise known as the method of residues. The following outline of "The Answer to Korea" uses an implicative order of topics.

I. Four possible solutions
   A. Truman's policy
   B. Use of A-bomb
   C. Withdrawal
   D. MacArthur's plan
II. Truman's unwise policy of localizing the Korean war
   A. No progress made
   B. Communist troops poured in indefinitely
   C. Involvement of more than Korea
III. Risk in use of A-bomb
   A. Costly in lives and cities
   B. Problem of where to bomb
   C. Grave risk of retaliation on United States
IV. Withdrawal spelling defeat
   A. Appeasement
   B. Wastes the lives and treasure already spent

So much for the theory of the implicative order, but what has been learned through experimental research about the wisdom of implying a conclusion instead of divulging it explicitly? Hovland and Mandell[8] found a very large difference in favor of the version of the speech in which the speaker drew the conclusion explicitly for the audience. In fact, more than twice as many listeners changed their opinions in the direction favored by the speaker when he stated his conclusion instead of implying it. The influences of the speaker's credibility, the sophistication of the audience, personality traits, and kinds of issues have not been fully explored. Tucker[9] found his version of the implicative order to be slightly more persuasive than the didactic with doubtful or opposed listeners, but this finding must be qualified by the knowledge that the conclusion was not strictly implied; the proposition was stated in the conclusion instead of in the introduction.

[8]C. I. Hovland and W. Mandell, "An Experimental Comparison of Conclusion-Drawing by the Communicator and by the Audience," **Journal of Abnormal and Social Psychology,** 47, 3 (July 1952), 581–588.
[9]Raymond Tucker, "Effects of the Implicative Sequence in Persuasion," unpublished doctoral dissertation, Northwestern University, 1956.

Indirect order, which is also called "inductive," is said to be more persuasive with doubtful and hostile listeners. Some advocates have found the traditional format of logical outlining to be psychologically unsatisfactory, because it sets out conclusions before it presents their support. The preceding specimen outlines on world government and civil-service reform are examples of that so-called "deductive" order. In their attempts to minimize the shock of an unpopular conclusion, some advocates have used an inverted arrangement of each topic. This scheme is erroneously called "inductive"; it is simply an indirect approach. It is accomplished either by means of a series of illustrations followed by a conclusion, or by an inverted enthymematic structure.

The following indirect-order outline enabled a classroom speaker to reach a conclusion by means of the latter structure.

"Who Should Judge?"

1. DU Fraternity
   a. Hazed pledges
   b. Fraternity put on probation by administration
2. Triangle Fraternity
   a. Pledge "walkout"
   b. Fraternity put on probation by administration
3. Sigma Chi Fraternity
   a. Pledge "hell week"
   b. Fraternity put on complete probation by administration
4. Kappa Kappa Gamma Sorority
   a. Senior class "walkout"
   b. Two school functions canceled by administration

A. All disciplinary actions concerning Greek organizations have been taken by the administration alone.
   1. SAE lion-painting case is one illustration.
      a. Two boys were caught painting the SAE lions.
      b. Administration suspended them for ten days.
   2. **Daily**-stealing case is another example.
      a. Three boys were caught stealing a day's issue of the **Daily**.
      b. Administration suspended them for ten days.

B. All disciplinary actions concerning individuals have been taken by the administration alone.
   1. Minnesota has a student judiciary.
   2. Michigan has a student judiciary.

3. Purdue has a student judiciary.
C. At least three comparable institutions have student judiciaries that assist the faculty in solving disciplinary problems.
  I. We ought to try the student-judiciary plan.

Problem-solution order is frequently used in deliberative (persuasive) speaking on proposed actions. Speeches that advocate propositions of policy, either in legislative or in oratorical contest situations, commonly point up problems and recommend solutions. Some writers refer to this as the disease-remedy pattern. The chief problem in using this order is that of proportion. Common sense should prevent a speaker's spending more than half of his time on the statement of a problem that is well known to his audience. His solution, which is less familiar and more controversial, deserves more than the short treatment it frequently receives. The major emphasis should be given to the problem phase only in case the speaker can make his greater contribution there. Such may be the case when the audience either has not previously had the advantage of a penetrating analysis of the problem or has not realized the seriousness of the need for action.

Altgeld's "Unnecessary Imprisonment" is an example of a double problem-solution order. First, he said there were a great many persons sent to prison simply because they could not pay the fine for breaking an ordinance. He described in detail the ill effects of their being sent to Bridewell (in Chicago) to work out a fine. Instead of imprisonment, he proposed his first solution, namely, that an investigation be made into each case, and that, except in extreme cases, the sentence be suspended and the accused be released, to be free as long as he conducted himself properly.

Second, many persons were imprisoned, occasionally as long as a week, before the court could consider their cases, and then they were released without sentence when no evidence of legal offense was found. To avoid this type of unnecessary imprisonment, Altgeld recommended his next solution, namely, that these persons not be held unless the protection of society required it. He deplored the custom of arresting as many as possible, and urged a more kindly feeling between the police and the poor and the outcast.

There is some disagreement over which should be stated first, the need or the plan. One experiment[10] showed that the need-plan order is more persuasive among persons with a relatively weak desire for understanding, while those who want to get the message do not need to hear the "need" point before the "plan." In general, the safer course is to begin with need-arousal unless the speaker knows his listeners are already interested.

Pro-and-con order is used when one advocate presents not only his own side but also some arguments for the opposing side. Is it more persuasive to use the pro-and-con order, or is one-sided presentation better? Might not the presentation of the "other" side cancel the effect of the speaker's case? These questions have been investigated experimentally. Three behavioral scientists used fifteen-minute talks, some one-sided and some two-sided, after which they measured the immediate effects. Among the men initially opposed to the speaker's proposition, the one-sided arguments produced a shift of 36 per cent toward the speaker's view, while the two-sided shifted 48 per cent. Among the men initially favorable, the one-sided shifted 52 per cent, while the two-sided moved only 23 per cent. Thus the two-sided order was superior among the listeners who were initially opposed to the speaker's position. Educational level of listeners made a difference, too. The two-sided was more persuasive among the better-educated men, but the one-sided succeeded better with the less educated.[11]

But what if opposing arguments in the form of counterpropaganda were given later? Would the one-sided or the two-sided presentations build the greater resistance to counterpropaganda? Two experimentalists measured the difference between the one-sided and the two-sided presentations in terms of the subsequent resistance to counter-propaganda. Three findings were announced: (1) the two-sided was more effective (59 per cent to 5 per cent) regardless of initial opinions; (2) the two-sided was more influential among the initially opposed; (3) the one-sided was more effective among the initially favorable who were not exposed to counterpropaganda.[12]

Finally, there is a study that tested the comparative persuasive-

[10]A. R. Cohen, "Need for Cognition and Order of Communication as Determinants of Opinion Change" in **Yale Studies in Attitude and Communication,** Vol. I, ed. C. I. Hovland (New Haven: Yale University Press, 1957), pp. 79–97.

[11]C. I. Hovland, A. A. Lumsdaine, and F. D. Sheffield, **Experiments on Mass Communication,** (Princeton: Princeton University Press, 1949).

[12]C. I. Hovland, I. L. Janis, and H. H. Kelley, **Communications and Persuasion** (New Haven: Yale University Press, 1953), pp. 108–110.

ness of one-sided and two-sided presentations of argumentative speeches and compared the effectiveness of three methods of organizing the latter.[13] Four original, recorded speeches were developed as follows: one-sided for the speaker's position, two-sided in a climax order, two-sided in anticlimax order, and two-sided in an interwoven order. The "other side" was presented late in the climax order, early in the anticlimax, and mixed into the interwoven. All methods resulted in significant shifting of opinions, but **relative** effectiveness among the four methods of arrangement was observable only in the "favorable" listeners. The specific findings were six: (1) two-sided climax order was more effective than the one-sided; (2) two-sided climax was better than the two-sided anticlimax; (3) two-sided interwoven was better than the two-sided anticlimax; (4) two-sided interwoven was better than the one-sided; (5) two-sided anticlimax and the one-sided differed little; (6) two-sided climax and two-sided interwoven differed little.

Climax and anticlimax orders are still involved in theoretical and scientific disputes. Much of the controversy stems from differences in definition. Some writers think of climax order as a matter of emphasis by space, while others mean the emotional climax or the high point of interest. No one seriously advocates a psychological anticlimax pattern in which the speech "fizzles out" at the end. Those who favor the so-called "anticlimax" order mean that the point that receives the **longest** treatment should come first. Their premise is that the length of a topic is a sign of its importance. Since effective speakers aim at an **emotional** climax in persuasive discourse, the only real problem is where to put the longest topic.

It may, therefore, be useful to distinguish between the two orders on the basis of primacy **versus** recency. According to the law of primacy, the longest, most important topic in the speech body should come first. According to the law of recency, the longest, most important point should come last. Fosdick used the primacy principle, which means that the longest topic came first in the body of his sermons. He has said that he aimed at a cumulative, emotional climax, even though he followed the law of primacy. His sermon structure differed from that of numerous other ministers in

[13]J. A. Jaska, "An Experimental Study of One-Sided and Two-Sided Argument with Emphasis on Three Two-Sided Speeches," abstract of dissertation in **Speech Monographs,** XXXI (August 1964), 234.

that his three-point development was (a) long point, (b) medium-length point, and (c) short point, while theirs was short-medium-long.

Two versions of the "skyrocket" speech pose an interesting problem in this connection. Sarett and Foster define it as a story-and-moral format, in which case the moral is the more important but should be placed last in order.[14] The climax in terms of emotional impact and forcefulness in delivery should, of course, come on the last point. Luccock's "skyrocket" sermon pattern contains a life problem, a spiritual truth, and a solution to the problem.[15] The cumulative, emotional climax comes near the end, but the first point may in some cases require the longest treatment.

Apparently the rhetorical theorists differ in their evaluation of the comparative advantages of the climax and the anticlimax patterns of arrangement, probably because of different definitions and the confusing effect of the primacy-recency dispute. This dispute will be taken up separately near the end of this chapter.

What are the published results of experimental research on the climax-anticlimax problem? Here again the primacy-recency dispute muddies the waters. Two investigators asked the question, "When an advocate presents only his side of a proposition, should he place his strongest point first or last?" Sponberg [16] found an advantage in favor of the anticlimax order within a **single** speech, but Cromwell,[17] who used **two** speeches on the one side, found the opposite result. One difficulty is that the former defined strength as length, whereas the latter defined it as convincingness. Also, the factor of audience interest may make a real difference. McGuire[18] raised a related but different question, "When predicting both pleasant and unpleasant contingencies, which should come first?" In a non-oral communication, he found it better to place the pleasant prediction first, because placing a punishing experience in first position results in avoidance

[14]L. Sarett and W. T. Foster, **Basic Principles of Speech** (Boston: Houghton Mifflin, 1946), p. 283.
[15]H. E. Luccock, **In the Minister's Workshop** (New York: Abingdon-Cokesbury, 1944), p. 140.
[16]H. Sponberg, "A Study of the Relative Effectiveness of Climax and Anticlimax Order in an Argumentative Speech," **Speech Monographs**, XIII (1946), 35–44.
[17]H. Cromwell, "The Relative Effect of Audience Attitude of the First Versus the Second Argumentative Speech of a Series," **Speech Monographs**, XVII (1950), 105–122.
[18]William J. McGuire, "Order of Presentation as a Factor in 'Conditioning' Persuasiveness," in **Yale Studies in Attitude and Communication**, Vol. I, ed. C. I. Hovland (New Haven: Yale University Press, 1957), pp. 98–114.

training. There is some basis for believing that the effect of prior messages upon later ones will be determined by the rewarding or the punishing nature of the first communication.

Gulley and Berlo[19] investigated some variations of the climax-anticlimax question. They noted that five earlier studies of retention of information were contradictory and inconclusive with respect to the advantage of the first or last position in a series of points, or of a climax or an anticlimax order. Further, they pointed out that three earlier studies showed a slight superiority of a climax order in terms of attitude change. In their own study, they limited their conclusions to aurally perceived messages. Their first question was, "Are there significant differences among climax, anticlimax, and pyramidal structures as revealed in attitude change?" Climax order proved to be the best, but not significantly so. Their second query turned up the finding of no difference in retention of communicated material. These conclusions relate to structures of individual arguments, not a series.

Causal-relations orders are often used in predicting consequences and in placing blame. Explanations and arguments can be based upon a progression that may be from cause to effect or vice versa. If the object is to point out why a present condition exists, the effect-to-cause order is indicated. If, on the other hand, a prediction is to be made concerning the future consequences of a present situation, the cause-to-effect order should be used. The direction of the reasoning should be from the known to the unknown, or from the admitted to the controversial.

The following summary illustrates the effect-to-cause order:

(*Effects*)	(*Causes*)
1. Ginny Lee Myers was killed by an automobile while crossing a street.	1. Insurance company records prove that speed is a major cause in most traffic fatalities.
2. Automobile accidents occupied more space on the front page of the Lincoln **State Journal** and the Omaha **World Herald** than any other news item.	2. The use of alcohol has become a social necessity in some communities.

[19]H. E. Gulley and D. K. Berlo, "Effect of Intercellular and Intracellular Speech Structure on Attitude Change and Learning," **Speech Monographs,** XXIII (November 1956), 288–297.

3. One person is injured in an automobile accident every three seconds; one person is killed in motor accidents every one and one-half minutes.

3. Car is still subject to mechanical failure.

4. Last year, 1492 persons met death at railroad crossings.

4. We still have bad crossings, unmarked grades, and bad weather.

The next summary illustrates the cause-to-effect order:

(*Cause*)	(*Effect*)
Conventional and traditional attitudes (such as snobbery) of one social set of girls toward others.	Maladjustment of these girls to social life.

Increasing-difficulty orders are peculiarly suited to informative speeches. Either the simple-to-complex or the familiar-to-unfamiliar pattern is a likely choice. The obvious reasons are that these patterns facilitate understanding and minimize the risk of discouraging the learners.

A speaker should beware of giving his listeners more than they can digest or of allowing their interest to wane. He must realize that they will be offended if he labors the simple and the obvious. It is well to use familiar illustrations throughout the speech and to conclude with relatively easy material. Doing so will relax the strain and enable most persons to leave with the satisfaction of having learned something.

The following structure-substance outline shows how Joseph Louis Lagrange used an increasing-difficulty pattern of arrangement in his lecture "On Arithmetic, and in Particular Fractions and Logarithms" in 1795:

Introduction—Systems of numeration and definition of scope of this lecture.

I. Fractions
    a. Greatest common divisor   *Familiar* a *leads to unfamiliar* b.
    b. Continued fractions   *Fairly easy* 1 *proceeds to more diffi-*
       (1) Expression   *cult* 2 *and then into very difficult* 3.
       (2) Termination
       (3) Convergents
       (4) Origin   *4 is comparatively simple.*

II. Theory of Powers, Proportions,
    and Progressions
 a. Proportions   *Increasing-difficulty device used for*
  (1) Arithmetical   *both headings and subheadings.*
  (2) Geometrical
 b. Progressions
 c. Involution and Evolution
 d. Compound Interest
 e. Annuities
III. Logarithms   *Difficult* c *is preceded by less diffi-*
 a. Invention by Napier   *cult* a *and* b, *followed by easy* d.
 b. Origin in mathematics
 c. Computation
 d. Use and necessity
Conclusion—Value of the history of *The closing is not difficult, and pro-*
science   *vides a tapered ending, clear to the*
               novice.

Topical-classification order is based upon the association of ideas. It sets out the several facets of a subject, points out various ways to meet a problem, or classifies general matter into categories. The "jewel" pattern, as some writers call it, turns an idea around so that each facet reflects light. An outline based upon the economic, political, and social aspects of a subject is a case in point. The classification device appeared in a John H. Holmes sermon on the three kinds of people among the Israelites in their desert march: those who wanted to return to Egypt, those who were satisfied wherever they were at night, and those, including Moses, who were determined to push on.

Two sketchy outlines, one key-phrase and one sentence, illustrate some beginning speakers' acceptable attempts at topical-classification arrangement:

"Chicago's Offerings"

 I. The educational possibilities
 II. The social aspect
 III. Sports
 IV. Business opportunities
 V. Professional aspects
 VI. Job prospects

"Relief for the Panhandle"
I. Why is the Panhandle a thirsty region?
II. What can be done?
III. How can money be obtained?
IV. Who can obtain the financial aid?
V. When can the money be obtained?

Extended-analogy order in speech is comparable with allegory in literature. It involves a long comparison that extends throughout a discourse. As has been said of analogical reasoning, this pattern of thought and of arrangement is excellent for illustrations but risky as proof. The following précis represents the use of extended analogy in a classroom speech:

> The lives of some public leaders remind us of the growth of rivers. As mighty rivers start in babbling brooks, so powerful men begin as helpless babies. Brooks grow into rivers, gaining power, becoming unruly, and sometimes destroying by erosion and floods. When men grow powerful, they may lose the idea of good and turn to doing harm.
>
> But the Nile does not follow such a course; it is a producer rather than a destroyer. Our public figures should follow its example.

The recency-primacy dispute has engaged the interest of theorists and experimenters for at least forty years. It is a question of crucial importance, because the facts of this matter will influence every scheme of arrangement that can be suggested. Basically the question is this: Will an idea be retained longer and exert more influence if it is the most recently perceived, or will it fare better if it is the first of its group to be perceived? The theorists' answers to this complex question can be inferred from the patterns of arrangement that have been explained above. The following paragraphs will show what the experimental studies have contributed toward answering the question.

Hovland, Janis, and Kelley[20] posed this question: "When two sides of a controversy are presented successively, does the first or the latter have an advantage?" They first cited the conclusions of four earlier studies: Lund in 1925 called his findings the "law of primacy"; Knower's 1936 study is often quoted in support of primacy;

[20] C. I. Hovland, I. L. Janis, and H. H. Kelley, **Communication and Persuasion** (New Haven: Yale University Press, 1953), pp. 120–133.

Cromwell in 1950 favored recency; as did Hovland and Mandell in 1952. This survey by Hovland, Janis, and Kelley expressed doubt that it will ever be meaningful to postulate a "law of primacy." It would be wiser to weigh the influences of motivation to learn, associative factors, attitudes towards the communicators, commitment and self-consistency, and initial attitude, for instance.

Reporting in 1946, Sponberg[21] favored primacy. He found that the arguments presented first were retained longer and were more persuasive than those presented last.

Obviously some intervening event between the first and the last presentations might make a difference. Hovland, Campbell, and Brock[22] asked what would happen if listeners were to hear one side, then make a public commitment to that side, and finally listen to the opposite side. They found that the act of commitment to the first presentation builds resistance to the opposing arguments, as shown in the reduction in shifts to the second presentation.

Using a "pro" argument before a "con" in a single, written communication, Janis and Feierabend[23] found support for the primacy hypothesis. However, the rival arguments were not contradictory; one side might use "need" whereas the other might use a "plan" or "advantages" argument. Luchins[24] likewise found primacy to be more pronounced than recency in several written-communication situations.

Finally, there is a published study that suggests that the recency-primacy dispute has been waged on the wrong ground. It will be recalled that Hovland in the **Yale Studies** ruled out completely any general principle of primacy in persuasion but specified some conditions favoring primacy. Miller and Campbell[25] interpret their findings to mean that there is a pervasive principle, the negatively accelerated forgetting curve of Ebbinghaus (1913), which generates

[21]H. Sponberg, "A Study of the Relative Effectiveness of Climax and Anticlimax Order in an Argumentative Speech," **Speech Monographs,** XIII (1946), 35–44.
[22]C. I. Hovland, E. H. Campbell, and T. Brock, "The Effects of 'Commitment' on Opinion Change Following Communication," in **Yale Studies in Attitude and Communication,** Vol. I, ed. C. I. Hovland (New Haven: Yale University Press, 1957), pp. 23–32.
[23]I. L. Janis and R. L. Feierabend, "Effects of Alternative Ways of Ordering Pro and Con Arguments in Persuasive Communications," **ibid.,** pp. 115–128.
[24]A. S. Luchins, "Primacy-Recency in Impression Formation," **ibid.,** pp. 33–61.
[25]N. Miller and D. T. Campbell, "Recency and Primacy in Persuasion as a Factor of the Timing of Speeches and Measurements," **Journal of Abnormal and Social Psychology,** LIX (July 1959), 1–9.

recency effects. The apparent primacy effect stems from Jost's second law, which states that of two equally strong associations at a given point in time, the older will decay less rapidly. Furthermore, the effect of delay in measurement upon the relative strength of the first and second messages must be considered. Miller and Campbell conclude that coming first (primacy) gives a statement no greater likelihood of being remembered, but it does improve its credibility.[26] Recency does not exclude primacy, apparently. The implication seems to be that the speaker's favorite point should come first but that it must be stated attractively and reviewed at the end so that it will be both credible and memorable.

ASSIGNMENTS

1. Prepare a topical phrase outline of a speech to inform. Use one of these patterns of arrangement: time, space, increasing-difficulty, or topical classification.
2. Prepare a logical sentence outline of a speech to persuade. Give the specific purpose and the anticipated audience attitudes. Use evidence, reasoning, and the appropriate connectives.
3. Convert a logical sentence outline into a presentation outline, using either an implicative or an indirect order of arrangement.
4. Discuss the practicability as well as the theoretical soundness of the nine "persuasive designs" that the article referred to in footnote 7 lists.
5. Analyze a written or an oral speech for the purpose of determining its pattern of arrangement.
6. Suggest some speech situations for which each of the patterns of arrangement would be appropriate.

[26] The Miller-Campbell study used the untested assumption that retention produces opinion. See C. A. Insko, "Primacy Versus Recency In Persuasion as a Function of the Timing of Arguments and Measures," **Journal of Abnormal and Social Psychology,** LXIX (October 1964), 381–391.

SIX

Introductions, conclusions, and transitions

Introductions

The functions of an introduction are to establish contact with the audience, to provide a background, to divulge and limit the theme and purpose, and to make a transition to the body of the speech. These somewhat specific functions of an introduction aid in the fulfillment of the general function, which is to introduce the speaker himself and his message to the audience.

It is well known that the problem of establishing contact varies with the kinds of audiences and their dominant attitudes. A casual audience on a street corner is more difficult to polarize than an organized audience in an established meeting place. It is equally obvious that a friendly audience presents almost no problem of establishing contact; whereas indifferent, doubtful, and hostile audiences pose problems in varying degrees of severity.

In many situations a speaker's first job may be the gaining of attention and good will. The audience may be indifferent, curious, friendly, doubtful, or hostile; but most persons will listen at least for a minute or two before their initial curiosity wanes. The devices and the kinds of introductions described below have been found to

70

be of value in gaining and holding attention and interest. The chief problem in establishing contact is that of adapting to the dominant attitudes that audience analysis has revealed. Observe the practices of a few expert speakers in this connection.

Webster adapted his topical sequence to audience attitudes in the following and in other similar deliberative speeches. His topical sequence in "The Revolution in Greece" was intended to win over an indifferent or a mildly hostile audience. In the introduction, he disclaimed any attempt at display, saying he proposed to show the effects of the Greek affair upon the institutions of free government. Following this, he met two objections that accounted for the attitude of opposition in his audience: the belief that the resolution was purely political, and the fear of foreign involvement.

A modern example will serve to illustrate the use of a disarming technique in dealing with attitudes of doubt and opposition. In 1944, while he was in charge of the Office of Price Administration, Chester Bowles had occasion to defend his program before the Senate Banking and Currency Committee. At the outset, he disarmed his listeners by acknowledging the unpopularity of the O.P.A., admitting its past mistakes, and assuring the senators that these faults were being corrected. He pointed out in detail why these flaws came about because of necessary haste, inexperienced personnel, and the enormous size of the job. Several newsmen credited him with putting his prospects in a "mellow, receptive mood."

Hostility in audiences has been met in a number of ways. One of these is by means of conciliation, as in the Bowles example. Other techniques have included complimenting the audience, appealing for a fair hearing, showing the prejudice to be ill-founded, and by establishing a common bond of interest, belief, and sympathy. The introduction of Beecher's Liverpool speech is perhaps the most familiar instance of an appeal for fair play:

> It is a matter of very little consequence to me, personally, whether I speak here to-night or not. But one thing is very certain, if you do permit me to speak here to-night, you will hear very plain talking. You will not find me to be a man that dared to speak about Great Britain three thousand miles off, and then is afraid to speak to Great Britain when he stands on her shores. And if I do not mistake the tone and temper of Englishmen, they had rather have a man who opposes them in a manly way than a sneak that agrees with them in an unmanly way. Now, if I can carry you with me by sound convictions, I shall be

immensely glad; but if I cannot carry you with me by facts and sound arguments, I do not wish you to go with me at all; and all that I ask is simply **fair play.**

Some speakers have met hostility with open defiance. This was the technique of George William Curtis in the Republican convention of 1860. When Curtis arose to speak, his voice was drowned by an uproar from the opposition. He folded his arms, calmly faced the noisy crowd, and waited. When they quieted down out of curiosity, he announced that he had a few words to say, and that he was determined to say them "if I stand here until tomorrow morning."

Student speakers seldom encounter such hostile audiences. They are more likely to meet indifference. Consequently, their chief problem is how to be interesting. They must usually clarify ideas, exert some effort to make their ideas interesting, and, in general, "put their best foot forward." They must occasionally establish their authority to speak, but they are less often obliged to conciliate a hostile audience.

Almost any speaker who is competently introduced and who approaches his audience with a confident manner can count on audience attention, unless the gathering is casual and disorganized. The fact that attention is given at the outset is no assurance that the speaker can retain it without effort. Bryan observed that Phillips and Conwell made conscious efforts to gain attention in their introductions, and he deliberately emulated them. Many other successful speakers have followed the same practice. President Truman opened a nationwide address on economic controls with this bid for attention: "I am going to talk to you tonight about a real, practical down-to-earth problem that affects the daily life of every American. It affects your savings, your pocketbook and your standard of living."

This quoted passage is an example of the attention device known as self-interest or an appeal to the vital. Other interest and attention devices include adaptations to audience attitudes, references to the closeness of the problem to the individuals present, illustrations dealing with prominent or unusual persons, allusions to audience experiences, and the use of materials that satisfy human interest in novelty, suspense, conflict, activity, stories, pictures, and humor. All of these devices are used to motivate attention. They provide reasons for listening to a speaker. Closeness or proximity is used in the form of a reference to someone who is present, or a statement to show that the problem of the speech is near at hand or imminent. Narrative introductions derive their impact from their utilization of human interest in unusual things, uncertain outcomes as in mysteries, conflicts between opposing forces, exciting action, vivid imagery, and humor. Because most of these factors of interest and attention are featured in some of the following kinds of introductions, they require no further elaboration here.

An introduction should contain, in addition to materials to secure attention and good will, such background as the audience may need. Sometimes none is required, but there are situations that require the speaker to define terms, explain his method of analysis, and sketch the origin and development of the problem. With the attention of the audience polarized, the speaker's second problem is that of preparing the listeners to understand his message. The amount of preparation varies among subjects and audiences, but the principle is that the auditors must have enough background to understand what is said. That is why first affirmative speeches in school debates usually begin with definition and history. In the wartime addresses of Roosevelt and Churchill, for example, there were many introductory paragraphs to shape a background context for the proposals that followed. One of the longest of these reviews was in Churchill's address to Commons on January 18, 1945. It began:

> I gathered that it was the desire of the House that there should be a further discussion of the war and foreign situations and policies at this time and before any new important international conferences take place. I will try to survey the whole of this, or a large and selected portion of this vast scene, to the best of my ability.

A third possible function of an introduction is to divulge the theme, limit the scope of the address, and perhaps to state the purpose. Listeners do not expect to wait very long for a statement of the speaker's central idea and his purpose. Unless there is some compelling reason for withholding the purpose for a time, the introduction should reveal and clarify the subject and the purpose in using it. This may be called the orientation of the audience. Wilson often clarified his purpose early in the introduction. In his address

"Loyalty Means Self-Sacrifice," delivered before the Conference on Americanization in 1916, he stated his purpose at once:

> I have come here for the simple purpose of expressing my very deep interest in what these conferences are intendd to attain. It is not fair to the great multitudes of hopeful men and women who press into this country from other countries that we should leave them without that friendly and intimate instruction which will enable them very soon after they come to find out what America is like at heart and what America is intended for among the nations of the world.

It will be recalled that the first function of an introduction **may be** to gain attention and good will. In other words, this step is not always required. If the speaker and his audience are on good terms before he speaks, there is no problem of gaining good will. Furthermore, the fact that the persons choose to come to hear a speaker usually indicates an interest. There remains, however, a problem of retaining or renewing that interest.

Introductions are of several kinds, one of which is called the personal reference. Those whose eminence or age commands respect can with better grace refer to themselves in relation to the occasion. If the speaker is a celebrity, his remarks about himself are a kind of news. In any case, personal reminiscences are communicated more effectively when presented with tact, taste, and perhaps a sense of humor. This kind of introduction is more common in informal talks or in situations characterized by hostility toward the speaker himself. In the latter case he may need to establish his credibility directly.

When a speaker introduces his speech with a reference to himself, it is better to avoid apologies ("I haven't had time to prepare"), bromidic remarks ("I am glad to be in Podunk, the garden spot of America"), and suggestions of egotism ("Although you technical students don't appreciate poetry, I'm going to show you what you've missed in sonnets").

Personal-reference introductions are not the most common, but they can be found in speeches by Wilson, Clay, Webster, Roosevelt, and others. This is how a student speaker began: "I have it here in my pocket. It isn't a strange-looking sheet. It's something that many of you will be getting in the very near future. . . . It is my draft notice."

Narrative introductions, which are the second kind, are frequently used in demonstrative or occasional speaking. Literary and historical illustrations and figurative analogies are presented in story form for the combined purposes of arousing interest and introducing the theme of the speech. This is akin to the parable technique. Sometimes the story material takes the form of a personal-experience narrative, in which case it is quite similar to the personal reference. The chief risk is that the connection between the story and the point may be farfetched. A college orator began: "For about two weeks we had been sleeping on the ground. Then suddenly, one day, our hospital ward tents arrived from the beach, and we were fortunate enough to obtain a new one. However, when we unfolded it, we discovered that all we had was a fly tent. . . . Three nights later a terrific wind and rain storm swept down on us. . . ."

Introductions that refer to audiences are the third kind to be treated here. They occur most often in informative and persuasive speeches. Speakers who use this kind of opening may begin by complimenting the audience or in some other way showing their appreciation of the group under whose auspices they speak. When done with good taste, this expression of good will signifies a speaker's awareness of the interests, attitudes, and motives of his listeners. This is particularly true when the speaker suggests a connection between his subject and their vocational, recreational, personal, or public interests. Because listeners of at least average sophistication are wary of fulsome expressions of pleasure, it is well to make such opening remarks simple and sincere. Seemingly any self-respecting speaker would refuse to stoop to cheap flattery. James Roosevelt employed a reference to his audience:

> It is a pleasure and an honor once again to appear before the Commonwealth Club. For nearly half a century this organization has demonstrated the value of open-minded inquiry, of unbiased discussion, and of a hard-headed determination to get the facts. These things must be preserved if we are to retain the key to progress.

Fourth, there is the reference-to-the-occasion introduction, which is fairly common among demonstrative speeches, although it occurs in other types. The speaker identifies himself with the audience by referring to the significance of the occasion or the circumstances that gave rise to the meeting. If the occasion is an anniversary, it is customary to point out some relationship between the subject and the date. In so doing, it is well to avoid the typical banalities of the Fourth of July, Memorial Day, and commencements.

Reference to the occasion often enables a speaker to motivate attention by pointing out some aspect of the occasion that makes the theme of the speech both timely and important. A reference to some item in the surroundings is another variation of this device. Such an adaptation should, of course, be brief and apt. A visiting speaker who addressed a school assembly on the values of traditions pointed to the banners and photographs on the wall as evidence of traditions in that high school. In this quotation from Harold Urey's talk on the hydrogen bomb and international government notice the reference to an anniversary: "I am happy to be addressing the members and friends of Americans for Democratic Action especially on the occasion of your Second Annual Roosevelt Day. The courage and daring of Franklin D. Roosevelt made possible the long gamble that led to the development of atomic power. . . ."

Fifth among the kinds of introductions is the reference to a quotation, to an incident, or to previous remarks. All of these references do not usually appear in one introduction, but opening statements containing one or more of them occur quite frequently. A recent, familiar event that has a close relationship to the speech subject is well worth using. Some of the most skillful parliamentary speakers, for example, are alert for opportunities to adapt to the remarks of previous speakers. Some of the best refutation and spontaneous humor stem from this situation. Any refutation, humor, or acknowledgment of a chairman's introduction should, of course, be magnanimous in spirit. Quotations, too, make good opening material, but they are not satisfactory substitutes for original ideas. They should be used as a familiar bridge to the theme of the speech. In all these references the relationship between the outside matter and the speaker's point should be clear rather than strained. The following example demonstrates an adaptation to a previous speech:

> Mr. President, I listened with great interest to the speech made to-day by the distinguished Senator from Iowa [Mr. Gillette]. I wish to assure the Senate that I have not consulted with the Senator from Iowa; but the arguments I shall make against the Atlantic Pact are very similar to the ones he made, and I agree thoroughly with the very

effective argument and very effective speech he made on that subject. However, the same arguments have led me to the conclusion that I must vote against the pact, rather than for it, as he has announced he intends to do.

Sixth, there is the humorous introduction, which is frequently misused. Too many speakers behave as if there were a rule that every speech must begin with a joke, regardless of its irrelevance to the subject or the occasion. It is debatable whether this fault is worse than oppressive seriousness. However, when the situation makes the light touch appropriate, audiences respond favorably to a pleasant, witty, or whimsical treatment of an idea, the audience, the occasion, or the speaker himself. Wit and humor are expected throughout some speeches of entertainment, but in a serious speech there is the risk of continuing the risible material to the point of obscuring the intended theme. Before using a humorous introduction, be sure it fits the point, suits the mood of the occasion, does not take more time than it is worth, and is a technique you can handle.

Some research has shown that the most effective classroom speakers use introductions that either contain humor or establish common ground. Audiences tend to remember clever introductions. One girl, who was describing life in a university-owned hotel, said, "Have you ever tried to say 'good night' to your date in a revolving door?" Lincoln often used anecdotes and quips in a similar fashion. Some speakers, including Tom Corwin and Mark Twain, had occasion to lament that they were taken as jokesters even when they had serious messages. Apparently there are two serious risks in the use of humor either in the introduction or elsewhere; it may be used to excess, and it may degenerate into vulgarity or some other violation of good taste.

The seventh kind of introductory portion of a speech is called a reference to the theme. It is most familiar in speeches to inform and to persuade. Because it plunges the audience into an immediate consideration of the subject, it is ill suited to hostile audiences. If a speaker starts with the history, timeliness, or meaning of his subject, he will be well advised to avoid a mere recitation of stale facts, needless details, dry explanations, and similar interest-killers. Factors of interest and attention need to be considered. A reference to the theme is not the simple business of saying, "To-day I am going to talk about foreign affairs." Something to motivate listening is needed here. John B. Gough, speaking on "Social Responsibilities" many years ago, referred to his theme in this way:

> The subject of this evening's address, as you all know, is "Social Responsibilities." There is a social responsibility that is recognized by society everywhere. The law of the land holds men responsible for the loss or injury to life or limb or property by malice, carelessness, or ignorance. . . . If a man throws a stone at a passing railway train, it will not do for him to say, "I did not think." . . . But there is a social responsibility recognized and enforced by the higher law of God—"Thou shalt love thy neighbor as thyself." It is of this responsibility that I would speak more particularly tonight.

Eighth in the list of introductions is the common bond, which has elements in common with the reference-to-the-audience. It is recommended in cases of resistance to a speaker's person or ideas. The procedure is to capitalize upon something the speaker and his audience have in common, such as beliefs, purposes, ancestry, traditions, or experiences. There is faint hope of success if a speaker fails at the outset to find an area of agreement with an otherwise doubting or hostile audience. In the following quotation from a student's speech we observe the common bond of childhood memories:

> In reminiscing over our younger childhood days, all of us have fond memories of that little gang we used to run around with. Perhaps out in the street, playing baseball or marbles. . . . But if we visualize that scene a little farther, we can see, off to one side of the playground, another little boy, standing there in deep anticipation with a strong hope that he might be asked to join the gang.

Finally, there is the introduction that utilizes a challenge or a paradox. In the presence of indifferent auditors, a speaker may need to arouse curiosity, shock them out of lethargy, puzzle them, or challenge them to meet an idea. President Butler of Columbia University used this kind of introduction in his commencement address, "The Insulated Life":

> There are comparatively few men and women alive in the world, although there are hundreds of millions of living human beings. The gap between a living human being and the man who is alive is far wider than the gap between the human being and the other primates,

although it is much more easily and quickly bridged by one who truly understands the arts of design and construction. The bridge which is so designed and constructed is conventionally described as a liberal education. . . .

Essential qualities of introductions include careful preparation, confident but modest tone, proper proportion, and interestingness. Because of the importance of the first impression, the introduction requires careful preparation. A speaker can get off to a smoother start and will be sure of saying what he intends if he will write his introduction and learn it. Although it comes first in a speech, the introduction should be prepared last. It is impossible to introduce accurately a discussion that has not yet been prepared.

In general, the opening statement should be correct in terms of facts, if any are used, and attractively worded. Farfetched, abrupt, and violent expressions are seldom appropriate. Finally, an introduction should be carefully wrought but simple.

A speaker who achieves modest confidence in his introduction steers a prudent course between the extremes of self-abasement and conceit. He neither apologizes nor boasts. In other words, he utilizes the force of positive suggestion to create a favorable impression of himself in the minds of his listeners.

This generalization should not, however, be taken to mean that all speakers must always refuse to explain their positions or to acknowledge their shortcomings. The following introduction from Wilson's "We Are Servants of the Rank and File of the People" goes further than necessary in this direction. Perhaps the audience felt so honored by the presence of the President that they overlooked the weak introduction. Student speakers should not go before audiences if their preparation has been such as to call for this expression of inadequacy.

> I realize that I have done a very impudent thing; I have come to address this thoughtful company of men without any preparation whatever. If I could have written as witty a speech as Mr. Pulitzer, I would have written it. If I could have written as clear an enunciation of the fundamental ideas of American patriotism as the mayor, I should have attempted it. If I could have been as appealing a person and of as feeling a heart as Mr. Cobb, I would have felt safe.
>
> If I could have been as generous and interesting and genuine as

Mr. Colby, I should have felt that I could let myself go without any preparation. But, gentlemen, as a matter of fact, I have been absorbed by the responsibilities which have been so frequently referred to here tonight, and that preoccupation has made it impossible for me to forecast even what you would like to hear me talk about.

How long should an introduction be? Examples vary from a few lines to a page or more. There is no definite rule, but experience indicates that the length should vary in terms of how much the listeners know, how they feel toward the speaker and his message, and the type of speech that is to be given. Some writers on homiletics advise using introductions that average between 5 and 15 per cent of the sermon length. A survey of 50 contemporary speeches shows the following average lengths of introductions in three types of speeches: 13 per cent in speeches to impress, 8.9 per cent in speeches to inform, and 7.5 per cent in speeches to convince.[1] However, there is a serious doubt that the average practice is the best practice. Longer introductions are obviously called for when ignorance, indifference, or hostility must be coped with. These difficulties are less likely to occur in situations where impressive speeches are given; therefore, shorter introductions should suffice.

Although the first section of this chapter has emphasized the importance of attention and interest in the introduction, this emphasis does not deny the importance of interestingness in **all** parts of a speech. It simply means that the **first** attempts to secure interest should be made in the introduction. "If you don't strike oil in three minutes, stop boring."

Conclusions

How long should a conclusion be? Some of the reported findings have shown the average to be approximately two-thirds the length of the average introduction. When the length of conclusions was compared with that of whole speeches, it was found that conclusions varied between 1 and 15 per cent of the speeches, the average being between 5 and 10 per cent.[2] These data were drawn from

[1]N. E. Miller, "Speech Introductions and Conclusions," **Quarterly Journal of Speech**, 32 (April 1946), 182.
[2]**Ibid.**

longer speeches than students usually present in class. If a student were to observe the average as reported here, he would spend between thirty seconds and one minute on the conclusion of a ten-minute speech. When the body of a typical classroom speech has served its function, a half-minute conclusion should suffice. In fact, some superior speeches have been concluded in one sentence.

Actually there is no firm rule governing the length of a conclusion. It is a variable that is affected by the kind of conclusion that is used and the function that it is intended to serve. The statistical comparisons that have been made indicate that the speeches with the shortest introductions have the shortest conclusions, and the speeches with the longest introductions have the longest conclusions. The length of both the introduction and the conclusion seems to vary in relation to the type and purpose of the speech. Among the speeches to convince and to inform, the conclusions average approximately 5 per cent of the total length. In speeches to impress, however, the conclusions are almost twice as long. The explanation is that inspirational material seems to require more lengthy treatment than do summaries, quotations, challenges, and the like.

Variations in the length and the content of conclusions can be observed in the Douglas campaign speeches in opposition to Lincoln. In Chicago, where he realized the futility of appealing for votes, Douglas concluded by thanking the audience for the reception he had received. At Bloomington, where he made a bid for support, his conclusion was three times as long as at Chicago. He identified himself with Webster, Clay, and the Union cause, and went on to request the voters' support if they considered him faithful to those principles. It is apparent that Douglas varied the length and content of his conclusions to meet the needs of each situation, just as he varied the arguments in the same speeches.

The functions of a conclusion are to point up main ideas, possibly to make a direct ethical appeal, possibly to appeal for action, and to provide a note of finality. With reference to persuasive speaking, Aristotle advised the use of four elements in conclusions: render the audience well-disposed to yourself and ill-disposed to your opponent; magnify and depreciate; put the audience into the right emotional state; refresh their memories. The conclusion says, in effect, "I have done; you all have heard; you have the facts; give your judgment." Each conclusion will do one or more of these things, depending upon the subject, the purpose, and the psychological state of the audience.

The function of pointing up the main ideas may apply to all kinds of speeches. This may be accomplished by means of a summary, a recapitulation, or an application of the ideas to a specific situation. These devices serve to put ideas in perspective and tie up loose ends. The importance of pointing up ideas is indicated by the fact that clear summaries have been found to distinguish the better classroom speeches. This does not mean that a conclusion must be definitive, because, as Gustave Flaubert pointed out in his **Letters,** humanity is forever on the march and can arrive at no goal. Homer, Shakespeare, Goethe, and the Bible, he asserted, came to no final conclusions. Student speakers will, therefore, do well to think of their conclusions as tentative.

Many eminent speakers have pointed up their main ideas in their conclusions. The Phillips eulogy of O'Connell is a case in point:

> When I consider O'Connell's personal disinterestedness—his rare, brave fidelity to every cause his principles covered, no matter how unpopular or how embarrassing to his main purpose—that clear, far-reaching vision and true heart which, on most moral and political questions, set him so much ahead of his times; his eloquence, almost equally effective in the courts, in the senate, and before the masses; that sagacity which set at naught the malignant vigilance of the whole imperial bar, watching thirty years for a misstep; when I remember that he invented his tools, and then measure his limited means with his vast success, bearing in mind its nature; when I see the sobriety and moderation with which he used his measureless power, and the lofty, generous purpose of his whole life,—I am ready to affirm that he was, all things considered, the greatest man the Irish race ever produced.

Reference has been made to direct ethos, which means a speaker's explicit reference to his own experience, sincerity, patriotism, or other evidences of character, intelligence, and good will. Such references may be made at any time in a speech, but only a speaker who still sensed some personal resentment toward himself late in his speech would have any real reason to make a direct ethical appeal in his conclusion. Darrow, Beecher, Schurz, and several other prominent speakers have been in this situation at times.

Burke, for instance, once said, "Let who will shrink back, I shall be found at my post." Darrow concluded his defense of Loeb and Leopold with this personal justification:

> I feel that I should apologize for the length of time I have taken. This case may not be as important as I think it is, and I am sure I do not need to tell this court, or to tell my friends that I would fight just as hard for the poor as for the rich. If I should succeed in saving these boys' lives and do nothing for the progress of the law, I should feel sad, indeed. If I can succeed, my greatest reward and my greatest hope will be that I have done something for the tens of thousands of other boys, for the countless unfortunates who must tread the same road in blind childhood that these poor boys have trod, that I have done something to help human understanding, to temper justice with mercy, to overcome hate with love.

Possibly in a majority of the speeches to secure action the speakers use conclusions that make appeals for specific, immediate action. Frequently the final emotional "push" is given here. The following conclusion from a classroom speech tells the audience what to do about the problem of accidents with firearms:

> But how does this affect you? The day will probably come when you will have to make a decision as to whether your child should be permitted to fire a gun. I want you and the thousands like you to make the right decision. So, until that time comes, go to your respective states this summer and acquaint the people there with this problem. Help to combat the attitude of indifference that prevails, so that they may act for the necessary legislation. And until that legislation is put into effect, practice the following safety advice: always keep guns dismantled and unloaded, out of the reach of smaller children, and always ask yourself whether your child is capable of handling a gun safely before you let him use it alone. Remember, it could happen to you!

Any conclusion should round out the speech and give it the effect of completeness. It should draw the speech together into a unified, impelling impression that will aid in the accomplishment of the speech purpose. This is the place to consolidate all of the impressions for the final impact. To end on a note of finality means to "quit all over," or to leave the audience with the feeling that what was begun has been accomplished. The specimen conclusions in the next section aptly illustrate this principle.

Eight kinds of conclusions are distinguished here. The "challenge" conclusion uses the device of the inspirational appeal, as in pointing to a struggle with a common foe: "Let's win the game," "Take up arms against the barbarians," and so on. It is one of the most frequently used kinds of conclusions. There was an element of challenge in the final line of one of Theodore Roosevelt's speeches: ". . . we stand at Armageddon, and we battle for the Lord." Wilson and Franklin D. Roosevelt used this kind of conclusion occasionally. A moderately-worded challenge appeared in the conclusion of a speech on the Japanese treaty by John Foster Dulles:

> In relation to Japan there is the opportunity to show which of the Allies of World War II now have the genuine will for peace. There is the opportunity for them to make a peace so righteous that the example will hearten and uplift men everywhere. That is the opportunity; and to its challenge we are determined worthily to respond.

There are times when it is effective to conclude with a quotation that is familiar or has the merit of expressing the intended idea better than the speaker can. This kind is almost as popular as the challenge. The quoted words of someone else must be consistent with the tone of the preceding material, and the passage should not be hackneyed. Among the favorite sources are poems, speeches, essays, plays, novels, and the Bible. Franklin D. Roosevelt used this type of conclusion in his speech "We Have Just Begun to Fight":

> We have need of that devotion today. It is that which makes it possible for government to persuade those who are mentally prepared to fight each other to go on instead, to work for and to sacrifice for each other. That is why we need to say with the Prophet, "What doth the Lord require of thee—but to do justly, to love mercy, and to walk humbly with thy God."

Repetition for the purpose of refreshing the listeners' memories is especially useful in speeches to influence belief. This is one of the three most popular kinds of conclusions. The list of topics may be reviewed in one of three kinds of summary statement: formal, paraphrased, and epigrammatic. Formal summaries occur in some forensic, legislative, and school-debate speeches. Characterized by a terse restatement of the body points in one-two-three order, the formal summary has no novelty or suggestive force. It is seldom a good kind to use, because mere reiteration is usually dull. It is better than none, however, if the speech has been long or complex. In his "Impeachment of Warren Hastings," Burke revived the recollection without repeating the speech:

> Therefore, it is with confidence that, ordered by the Commons,
>
> I impeach Warren Hastings, Esquire, of high crimes and misdemeanors.
>
> I impeach him in the name of the Commons, in Parliament assembled, whose parliamentary trust he has betrayed.
>
> I impeach him in the name of all the Commons of Great Britain, whose national character he has dishonored.
>
> I impeach him in the name of the people of India, whose laws, rights, and liberties he has subverted; whose properties he has destroyed; whose country he has laid waste and desolate.
>
> I impeach him in the name and by virtue of those eternal laws of justice which he has violated.
>
> I impeach him in the name of human nature itself, which he has cruelly outraged, injured, and oppressed, in both sexes, in every age, rank, situation, and condition of life.

Paraphrased summaries are sometimes used in order to avoid the risks of the formal type. These may take the form of the commonsense summary in which difficult concepts are expressed in everyday language. This kind of restatement in other words is more interesting, less abrupt, and more subtle than a formal summary. Webster employed this variety of informal summary in closing for the prosecution of the White murder case in 1830:

> Gentlemen, I have gone through with the evidence in this case, and have endeavored to state it plainly and fairly before you. I think there are conclusions to be drawn from it, the accuracy of which you cannot doubt. I think you cannot doubt that there was a conspiracy formed for the purpose of committing this murder, and who the conspirators were; that you cannot doubt that the Crowninshields and the Knapps were the parties in this conspiracy; that you cannot doubt that the prisoner at the bar knew that the murder was to be done on the night of the 6th of April; that you cannot doubt that the murderers of Captain White were the suspicious persons seen in and about Brown street on that night; that you cannot doubt that Richard Crowninshield was the perpetrator of this crime; that you cannot doubt that the prisoner at the bar was in Brown street on that night. If there, then

it must be by agreement, to countenance, to aid, the perpetrator, and, if so, then he is guilty as a principal.

Epigrammatic summaries are so named because they contain epigrams, which are short, pithy, and allegedly shrewd observations. Generally this device makes a trenchant conclusion. A statement such as "Fools rush in where angels fear to tread" has "punch" because it is short, vivid, seemingly wise, and easy to remember. Speaking about the importance of foreign trade to England, a winning student speaker concluded with this statement: "If foreign trade is the life blood of English economic life, we must help her prevent a hardening of the arteries."

Possibly the fourth kind in terms of popularity is the inspirational conclusion. In one version of this kind, the speaker inspires his followers by boldly taking the lead in using his own advice. In the other version, the speaker helps the audience to visualize better times ahead. He pictures the "new day" when his proposal will be making life beautiful for those who choose the proper course. To be sure, many so-called inspirational conclusions are trite and overdrawn, but they need not be so if they are conceived with taste and imagination. The first specimen, which is from Henry's "Liberty or Death" speech, illustrates the speaker's taking the lead in using his own advice; the second, from a speech by Harold Stassen, is the "new day" variety of inspirational conclusion.

> It is in vain, sir, to extenuate the matter. Gentlemen may cry, Peace, Peace—but there is no peace. The war is actually begun! The next gale that sweeps from the north will bring to our ears the clash of resounding arms! Our brethren are already in the field! Why stand we here idle? What is it that gentlemen wish? What would they have? Is life so dear, or peace so sweet, as to be purchased at the price of chains and slavery? Forbid it, Almighty God! I know not what course others may take; but, as for me, give me liberty or give me death.

> Some people say that our democracy is not perfect and that there is discrimination and inequality and apathy and corruption. They are right. Some say that our economic system has not functioned perdistributions. They are right.

> But neither of these facts is any reason for waiting for the correction of these imperfections before we step forward to fulfill the world leadership which it is mandatory that we exercise.

We must advance on both the world front and the domestic front at the same time. In fact, they are in large measure interdependent. I speak not of a utopia. I speak not of a human race suddenly turned angelic.

There will be selfishness and greed and corruption and narrowness and intolerance in the world tomorrow and tomorrow's tomorrow. But pray God, we may have the courage and the wisdom and the vision to raise a definite standard that will appeal to the best that is in man, and then strive mightily toward that goal.

In an emotional-appeal conclusion, a speaker uses Aristotle's principle that the audience should be put into a favorable emotional state for the appeal for belief or action. The idea is to make the audience **want** to agree by driving at the motive forces that lie in personal or local interests, emotional reactions, and the like. A rather personal sort of emotional appeal was used by both Clay and Churchill, as the following specimens indicate:

And, finally, Mr. President, I implore, as the best blessing which Heaven can bestow upon me upon earth, that if the direful and sad event of the dissolution of the Union shall happen, I may not survive to behold the sad and heart-rending spectacle.

Put your confidence in us. Give us your faith and your blessing, and, under Providence, all will be well.

We shall not fail or falter; we shall not weaken or tire. Neither the sudden shock of battle, nor the long-drawn trials of vigilance and exertion will wear us down. Give us the tools, and we will finish the job.

After a speaker presents a problem that he alleges to be serious, he should propose an adequate solution and advise the audience precisely what to do **now**. Each listener should be made to realize what his responsibilities and opportunities are. Do not leave unanswered the individual listener's question, "Where do I come in?" As we have observed earlier, this is a familiar weakness of problem-solution speeches, including college orations. This is how a classroom speaker attempted to advise his audience:

I think trucking is here to stay, but so is pleasure travel. So let's remember, the next time we hit a bone-jarring bump; the responsibility for it can be found. The trucking industry is beginning to get the blame as more and more people become conscious of the damage being done to public roads. The companies are putting all their efforts into a publicity campaign to "soft soap" the public. But as long as that public, us included, remembers the jarring we felt when we hit that hole in the road today, and as long as we remember the things that can be done to correct the situation, the trucking companies will be forced by public feeling and government action to take their just share of the responsibility for the condition of our highways. Now that we have the facts, we must blame ourselves if we don't demand action.

For the purpose of stimulating audience participation, at least on the subvocal level, in the thought process of the speech, the speaker may pose questions, rhetorical or otherwise. In some cases this is a method of stating a challenge. The principle is that provocative questions will involve the listeners personally in the concluding ideas. It is a device that is intended to induce your listeners to help you conclude the speech. One college orator opened her conclusion with these questions: "What do you think? What are you going to do about it?" Another speaker closed her oration with this question, "I, as a college sorority girl, resolve to do my part; do you?" Beveridge closed his speech "The Philippine Question" with this question, "How dare we delay when our soldiers' blood is flowing?"

The epitome conclusion suggests or echoes the whole speech by dramatizing ideas in an illustration or a capsule statement. It often portrays the central, abstract idea in a specific or a concrete way. Sander Vanocur closed his winning oration, "A State of Mind," in this way:

> We **must** have a new state of mind. I think that you and I must choose **our** states of mind, for **together** they are the state of mind of this nation. We must make our choice:
> It is human dignity or human misery.
> It is freedom or it is force.
> It is all a state of mind.

Near the end of his Pueblo speech on the League of Nations, Wilson used this illustration that epitomized his theme:

> My friends, on last Decoration Day I went to a beautiful hillside near Paris, where was located the cemetery of Suresnes, given over to the burial of the American dead. Behind me on the slopes was rank upon rank of living American soldiers, and lying before me upon the

levels of the plain was rank upon rank of departed American soldiers. Right by the side of the stand where I spoke there was a little group of French women who had adopted those graves, had made themselves mothers of those dear ghosts by putting flowers every day upon those graves, taking them as their own sons, their own beloved, because they had died in the same cause—France was free and the world was free because America had come! I wish some men in public life who are now opposing the settlement for which these men died could visit such a spot as that. I wish that the thought that comes out of those graves could penetrate their consciousness. I wish that they could feel the moral obligation that rests upon us not to go back on those boys, but to see the thing through, to see it through to the end and make good their redemption of the world. For nothing less depends upon this decision, nothing less than the liberation and salvation of the world.

There are a few cautions to observe. One is the advice against going on to a new point in the conclusion. The main reason is that a conclusion should secure a cumulative effect by drawing together the highlights of the body. If the final statement continued the work of the body, it is not a conclusion. This is analogous to the debate rule that no new line of argument may be introduced in a rebuttal speech.

Avoid the extremes of a tiresome summary and a flowery style. A formal summary adds little, if anything, to most speeches. It is equally true that a turgid flight of fancy has its risks, even though many demonstrative speakers have indulged in it. College students do not, as a rule, secure the desired response with this technique in classroom speeches. They are well advised to avoid imitating the typical Fourth-of-July orator.

Have no false conclusion. It often happens that a speaker goes on with sentence upon sentence after he has given an indication that he is about to conclude. The false conclusion makes the audience impatient, and it usually results in a weak conclusion anyway. This does not occur when a speaker writes and learns his conclusion.

Akin to this advice is the admonition to say no more than is necessary in the conclusion. Do not prolong it, lest it become tedious. There is no need for a long conclusion if the body has done its job. Textbook specimens from great speeches are frequently much longer than students should use in their short speeches. In many cases a sentence or two will suffice.

All of these cautions may be summarized with the statement, "Prepare carefully." The conclusion, like the introduction, should be written and learned. Since the final impression is important, a conclusion should not seem to be "tacked on." Only a conclusion that is carefully prepared can be counted on to serve one or more of the four important functions.

Transitions

A transitional sentence is a bridge from one idea to another in a speech. Most good speeches have several transitions. While it is true that the first major transition is likely to come at the end of the introduction, it is inaccurate to assume that linking sentences belong nowhere else. They should be used wherever there is an occasion to tighten the connections in a discourse. The typical transitional sentence looks backward and forward; it refers to what has just been said and then introduces the next idea. A major and a minor transition were used early in the Reverend Fulton J. Sheen's address, "Education As the Guardian of the American Heritage." The speaker concluded his first topic of definition with, "That is the American heritage." He moved to his next point by asking, "How does education preserve these rights and liabilities?" Upon finishing his topic concerning education as a developer of freedom, he said, "That tradition is freedom within the law and not outside of it." He moved to the next minor point with the statement, "Finally, education preserves the American heritage through the development of character." Note the transitions within the introduction and between the introduction and the body of Governor Warren's keynote speech before the Republican National Convention in 1944:

> We are here to do a job for the American people. And we mean business.
>
> What is our job? Ask any American. Ask the anxious American mother and father. Ask the anxious wives and sweethearts of our fighting men. Ask our fighting men themselves. They will tell you what our job is.
>
> They will give you the keynote for this convention. They will tell you out of their hearts and what they say will be the same—East and West, North and South, it will be the same.
>
> For now the same anxieties are on every American heart—the same

hour-to-hour concern for what the day may bring forth, the same steadfast courage to sustain them, the same dreams, the same hope that they will have a chance to make their dreams come true.

This is what is on their hearts. This is our job: . . .

ASSIGNMENTS

1. Select for critical analysis a few printed speeches. Which of the four functions of an introduction were apparently served?
2. Identify the kinds of introductions used in those reprinted speeches.
3. Evaluate the introductions in terms of the four essential qualities.
4. Write an introduction followed by a sketch of the ideas to be developed in your own speech. Using the structure-substance format, indicate the kind of introduction you have written, the functions it will serve, and its essential qualities. Include explanation and evidence to support your identification and appraisal. Indicate the type of speech as well as the estimated information and attitude of the audience. Why did you select a certain kind of introduction?
5. Practice composing transitional sentences for use between points in your own speech.
6. Again referring to the printed speeches, identify the functions served by the conclusions.
7. Identify the kinds of conclusions used.
8. Compose a conclusion for the speech in Assignment 4. Specify parenthetically at the end the kind of conclusion it is and its intended functions. Observe the cautions that were explained above.
9. A round of speeches might be followed by oral critiques emphasizing the principles relating to introductions, transitions, and conclusions.

Selected bibliography

In addition to the research items cited in footnotes, the following sources were consulted.

Arnold, C. C., Ehninger, D., and Gerber, J. **The Speaker's Resource Book.** Chicago: Scott, Foresman, 1961.

Ausubel, N., ed. **Voices of History (1945–46).** New York: Gramercy Publishing, 1946.

Baird, A. C., ed. **Representative American Speeches: 1949–1950.** New York: H. W. Wilson, 1950.

Brigance, W. N. **Classified Speech Models.** New York: F. S. Crofts, 1928.

Bryan, W. J. **The World's Famous Orations.** 10 vols. New York: Funk and Wagnalls, 1906.

Butler, N. M. **The Meaning of Education.** New York: Charles Scribner's Sons, 1915.

Churchill, W. S. **Blood, Sweat, and Tears.** New York: G. P. Putnam's Sons, 1941.

Congressional Globe, 31st Congress, 1st Session, Appendix I, pp. 115–127.

Congressional Record, 64th Congress, 1st Session, Vol. 53, p. 11925.

Copeland, L. **The World's Great Speeches.** New York: Garden City Publishing, 1942.

Faulkner, W. **The Faulkner Reader.** New York: Random House, 1954.

Fosdick, R. B. "The Challenge of Knowledge," **Vital Speeches,** (July 15, 1948), 586–587.

Highet, G. **People, Places, and Books.** New York: Oxford University Press, 1953.

Horner, J. K. **Elements of Public Speech.** New York: D. C. Heath, 1929.

James, H. **Charles W. Eliot.** Boston: Houghton Mifflin, 1930.

Lindgren, H. D. **Modern Speeches.** New York: F. S. Crofts, 1926.

Lutz, R. "The History of the Concept of Freedom," **Bulletin** of the A.A.U.P., (Spring 1950), 18–32.

McBurney, J. H., and Wrage, E. J. **The Art of Good Speech.** Englewood Cliffs: Prentice-Hall, 1953.

Mills, G. E. **Composing the Speech.** Englewood Cliffs: Prentice-Hall, 1952.

———. **Reason In Controversy.** Boston: Allyn and Bacon, 1964.

Monroe, A. **Principles and Types of Speech.** Chicago: Scott, Foresman, 1962.

Nesbit, W. D. **After Dinner Speeches.** Chicago: Reilly and Lee, 1927.

O'Neill, J. M. **Classified Models of Speech Composition.** New York: Century, 1921.

Reed, T. B. **Modern Eloquence.** 15 vols. Philadelphia: J. D. Morris, 1900.

Richardson, R. E. "The Speaking and Speeches of Jefferson Davis." Unpublished doctoral dissertation, Northwestern University, 1950.

Sarett, L., and Foster, W. T. **Basic Principles of Speech.** Boston: Houghton Mifflin, 1946.

———. **Modern Speeches on Basic Issues.** New York: Houghton Mifflin, 1939.

Thorndike, A. H., ed. **Modern Eloquence.** New York: Modern Eloquence, 1923.

Webster, D. **The Writings and Speeches of Daniel Webster,** National Edition. 18 vols. Boston: Little, Brown, 1903.

Wilson, J. F., and Arnold, C. C. **Public Speaking As a Liberal Art.** Boston: Allyn and Bacon, 1964.

Wilson, W. **The Messages and Papers of Woodrow Wilson.** Vol. I. New York: Review of Reviews, 1924.

———. **Selected Library and Political Papers and Addresses of Woodrow Wilson.** Vol. II. New York: Grosset and Dunlap, 1927.

Winning Orations: Interstate Oratorical Association. Evanston, Illinois, 1947 and 1950.

Winning Orations: Northern Oratorical League. Minneapolis: Northwestern Press, 1951.

Woodbridge, D. M. "John Peter Altgeld: A Spokesman for Democracy." Unpublished doctoral dissertation, Northwestern University, 1951.

Yeager, W. H. **Effective Speaking for Every Occasion.** Englewood Cliffs: Prentice-Hall, 1951.

Index

DATE DUE

F			
AR 23 '77			
AR 30 '77			